FROM THE LOFT

*Tales of a Former City Dweller
Living on a Horse Farm*

Copyright © 2016 by Greg Schaffer

All rights reserved.

No part of this book may be reproduced in any form or by any electronic or mechanical means including information storage and retrieval systems, without permission in writing from the author. The only exception is by a reviewer, who may quote short excerpts in a review.

This is a work of fiction. Names, characters, businesses, places, events and incidents are either the products of the author's imagination or used in a fictitious manner. Any resemblance to actual persons, living or dead, or actual events is purely coincidental.

Visit secondchancebook.org for more information on this and other titles from Second Chance Publishing.

ISBN - 978-0-9911052-0-5

11 10 9 8 7 6 5 4 3 2

Dedicated to round bale warriors everywhere.

Preface

From the Loft is a compilation of columns of the same name I wrote for a magazine called *The Horse Exchange* in the mid to late 2000s. The premise of those vignettes mirrored my personal life – a man who grew up in a city atmosphere (for me it was actually the suburbs of New York City) learning about life on a mini-farm with several horses to care for. Needless to say, I found some humor in my adjustment to the different agricultural lifestyle.

When the opportunity arose to pen a monthly (more or less) humor column for *The Horse Exchange*, I could not refuse. What, with so much material to pull from, the columns would almost write themselves. While fictional, loosely based on actual experiences, the light-hearted tales resonated with readers. The feedback I received was quite positive, even until the end. Yet, when *The Horse Exchange* folded in early 2009, so did *From the Loft*.

Or so I thought.

During one conversation not long ago with my mother, the column came up. I mentioned how great it would be to resurrect *From the Loft* as an anthology, but most of the original material was lost. Unfortunately, because of changes in computers and the disparate platforms that I used to write the columns over the years (some months I submitted only via email), I had copies of very few articles, and several of those were unreadable, given different word processing formats. I did not have sufficient material to produce a collective work, I explained to her.

How wrong I was. She had saved a print copy of nearly every column published!

It took significant effort to retype those paper copies, but it was worth it. When I compiled the first draft of all 42 columns (I believe that we collectively found them all), I saw a story emerging.

The anthology would happen, and here it is.

Most of the articles are very close to their original content, with minor style changes, presented roughly but not exactly in the order in which they originally appeared. Both of these changes help to establish a feel of consistency and continuity when compiled together.

Read, chuckle, and enjoy!

Greg Schaffer
December 2016

One
For Better and For Horse

My introduction to "all things equine" was via she who would become my wife, many years ago. Meeting her marked the beginning of my overall transformation from city dweller to country boy. I learned potatoes actually come from the ground, what a PTO is, and tossing hay up to a loft is not as easy as it looks, especially after hoisting seventy bales.

I sought to learn about horses as a means to impress her during our courtship. The way to a man's heart may pass through his stomach, but all roads to romance with a horse lover inevitably travel through hay and manure. Not long after our first date, I found myself cleaning stalls, filling water buckets, and measuring feed. I drew the line at deworming, although my fears were vanquished when I learned the product is designed to be administered orally, not, well, you know.

Those of us who are in the fraternity of men introduced through wedded bliss to the life of a horse lover understand truly just how passionate they are regarding anything horse related. I am fairly certain mine changed our vows slightly, as I am sure the minister said, "Do you promise to love and honor, for better and for horse . . ."

When we decided to spend an afternoon looking at houses shortly after our wedding, the differences in what we deemed important, must-have features for our next abode became obvious. The first place we looked at was spacious and had enough land for a few horses, over five acres. I was enthralled with the beautiful interior of the foyer and the great view from the large porch, while she inspected every inch of the barn and the fence line. I think it was about three days later when she realized the house actually came with the barn.

Convinced it was perfect for us and our two ponies, we purchased the place. While it took us some time to settle in completely – we were still unpacking six months later – she had set up the barn completely before I had returned the U-Haul.

Over the years, I've learned about accessories for the barn, some necessary, some, well, maybe more of a luxury. For example, while at a farm trade show the month before our pregnant mare was due to foal, we closely examined at one vendor booth wireless web cameras for barns, with the idea we could monitor the mare while we were away at work. Keep in mind this was circa 2003, and wireless Internet technology was still in its childhood.

I loved everything about the system except the price, and then I had a thought. "Honey, I can build a working setup for a fraction of this cost," I boldly proclaimed. Now, my wife over the years had learned to trust me more so than not when I offer such revelations, as I generally have found great success with these types of projects. Still, those rare times when my ideas have been, shall we say, flawed, are not far from her mind. Hey, in my defense, cooking homemade chicken soup, pasta and all, overnight in a crockpot seemed efficient, but if you try this at home, I guarantee you will not get soup. The product is great for spackling walls, though.

After some head scratching and tinkering with an old laptop, a web camera of the same vintage, and a wireless antenna made from a Pringles can, the video came on line, earning me some serious brownie points. I think my wife watched that poor mare constantly, and when she (our mare, not my wife) did eventually go into labor (we were there when it happened), I was tickled that several people were watching the beginning of the birthing live, over my set up. But as the labor progressed I became more enthralled about biology than technology, and never noticed the video feed went off line from too many hits. New life tends to change your focus, I guess.

So I think I've arrived, though not without some rocky spots, at being a competent horse hubby. The best compliment I received came a few months after the web cam phase, when one of my wife's friends, also a horse lover, remarked how natural I was with caring for the ponies. I'll be darned if somewhere along the way I actually became a horse lover, too. But don't tell my wife I actually enjoy cleaning stalls and throwing hay.

Two
Tic – TACK – Toe!

Early on in our courtship, I was quite eager to learn as much as possible about horses so I could better impress she who would become my wife. I figured horse care couldn't be too hard, and certainly the more time I spent in her world of muck buckets and hay strings, the less time I'd have to worry about traditional dating preparations such as shaving and showering. I was earning brownie points while looking like I just had finished shoveling manure (well, I usually had just finished shoveling manure). "This was as easy as tic-tac-toe!" I thought.

Well, nothing is as easy as it seems. One of my significant other's horses liked to play "hide the horse hockey" in her stall, and I never could figure out how to find a pee spot without tearing up every square inch of shavings. Adding to my dismay, I learned early on that showering and shaving prior to date night was in fact not optional, regardless of how many muck bucket loads I had transferred from the stalls to the manure spreader that afternoon. But, in some ways, the tic-tac-toe analogy still holds true.

Tic, rather ticks, are ugly blood sucking creatures that Hartz collars magically repel from cats. Ticks live in woods and tall grass, but the only woods that this former city dweller experienced growing up were the weeds and scrub trees that grew in the fence lines between houses that were built in the 60s, and generally all local residences had well-manicured lawns. Ticks were definitely not much of an issue in my childhood.

    My girlfriend boarded her horses locally, and that is where I learned the basic elements of horse care. Gathering the horses when it was time to put them up meant walking through fields where the grass sometimes had grown high enough to cover my sneakers and brush against my shins. On some days, the grass in the fields was shorter, and I wondered how long it took the owner of the property to push a Toro mower around to cut it. I had not yet been introduced to the concept of bush hogging, a topic for Advanced Horse Care 201.

    I remember vividly the first time when, after securing the ponies in their designated stalls, I discovered a new mole on my ankle. The realization of a new skin feature turned to horror when it moved. The "mole" turned out to be some alien-looking creature, a miniature black crab that just simply did not want to let go.

    Ticks weren't the only insects that were covered in my early equestrian education. Flies love horses, and I guess that's why they call the big ones that hang around them horse flies. Or maybe it's because they're huge. I learned early on not to get between flies and a horse's tail. When the horse whips that tail aiming at a fly, it is a deadly weapon. I considered wearing safety goggles around the ponies until the concept of "fly spray" was explained to me (Basic Horse Care 101).

Tac, rather tack, as in horse tack, was yet another concept that was alien to me before my introduction to equestrian life. I hadn't really thought much about equipment required to ride a horse before. What could be needed? Everyone who ever watched a John Wayne movie knew that you had to "saddle up" the horses before you rode them. Outside of that, giving them water from a well-placed and convenient stream in the middle of a desert, and tying them up loosely in front of the saloon at the end of a hard day herding cattle, punching outlaws, and cracking great one-liners, what else was there to operating a horse?

Again, my education was rapid. I learned in addition to the saddle, necessary accouterments included the girth, bit, stirrups, stirrup leathers, reins, saddle pads, and rear-end pads for the rider. Prepping a horse to ride was like dressing a kid for a winter's day trip to school – think of Randy in "A Christmas Story." Adjusting the girth in particular was difficult for me, just to get it tight enough so that the saddle wouldn't slip. To this day, I believe that when a horse sees me coming with a girth that magnificent creature puffs out its belly to make it that much harder to size the belt properly.

Learning how to tighten girths, though, had a practical application, as the methodologies I learned early in my "tacking up" days has served me well in dressing as my midsection has expanded with age. I still wear the same size pants I wore in college, it's just a little harder to convince the pants to close.

While tacking up a horse seems like a lengthy process, at least the shoes last many weeks, so that aspect of horse maintenance is not as frequent. Yet I learned that every now and then a horse "throws" a shoe, necessitating an unscheduled visit by a farrier to shoe the horse.

Let me be clear, by this point in time I was well educated enough to realize that the horse doesn't actually "throw" the shoe (horses play horseshoes?), but rather that the shoe would come off in the normal course of whatever a horse did during the day. Obviously, this is a major engineering defect. Shouldn't farriers use something besides nails to hold those shoes in place? Personally, I'd get out my Black and Decker cordless drill and countersink some quarter-inch wood screws. Maybe use some JB Weld between the shoes and the hoof as well. If I was a farrier, no horse would throw a shoe no matter what they did during their normal horse days.

As for the "toe" part of "tick – tac – toe," well, you never forget the first time your foot gets caught between a hoof and the ground. I still have an imprint from one of those farrier nails on my right big toe.

Three
Round and Round

My pre-equestrian involvement with and knowledge of hay was limited. As a kid, I liked hayrides, although sometimes the wagons had little actual straw on them. All I knew was that hay bales generally came in two types: small with corners and large, round mounds. Sort of like a Krystal burger (or a White Castle, for my friends up north) next to a Hardees 2/3 pound Angus Beef anchor.

Square (well, rectangular) bales are much lighter, but because they are smaller I tend to move square bales or flakes from such frequently. I calculated we move a single blade of hay from a square bale up to seven times. First, we load bales onto the truck. Then, to complete the stocking process, we toss bales from truck to loft and stack the hay in the loft.

Consumption rounds out the remaining four touches. We toss individual bales down to our feed room (so we don't have to go up to the loft every day) and stack the bales there. Finally, we put flakes out for feeding. Don't forget cleaning the stalls – moving waste qualifies as the seventh touch of hay.

Round bales eliminate some of those steps.

Typically, we don't use round bales except in the winter. The fields provide a good amount to eat during the warmer months, but after the growing season ends, the horses turn to other grazing sources.

During cold winter nights, our horses will lay their heads on top of a newly placed round bale and eat to stoke their heat-producing digestive furnaces. During the day, they'll lay in the chunks they've pulled away, enjoying the sun while nibbling on the hay on the ground. It looked comfortable so I tried something similar once at work with popcorn, but my boss was not too impressed.

My horse-loving half will occasionally come home with one of these round collections of overgrown grass sitting in the back of the truck, ready for the muscle half (me) to push it off for feeding time. I've long since come to accept that I tricked myself into this job – if I hadn't bought a truck, we wouldn't be able to haul hay. The amount we spent on the truck would have paid for a lot of hay deliveries, both the small and large varieties. At least I have saved money on a gym membership because of the excellent exercise I get moving hay from place to place.

So when I see the truck pulling in the driveway with a huge mound in the back, I know it's time to strap on the Carhartts and gloves and take an Advil or two before trudging to the field. I suppose if the bales were simply straw they would be fairly easy to move. These cylindrical monsters, however, are packed with all of the good stuff for growing and mature horses: vitamins, minerals, fiber, and pounds. All of that good stuff adds mass, and a good round bale can run a half a ton or more.

Now, from far away these things can look large, but up close you realize just how big these rolls are. The first time I planned to push a round bale off, I had some apprehensions about trying, but as the keeper of the Y chromosome in this partnership, this task of muscular power fell literally to my hands. As I sighed and tried to find a suitable position to get the most leverage, I was keenly aware that pain was better than humiliation from defeat, and that I'd better be able to push it off.

If the bale was oriented such that I could just roll it off, this would all be a moot point and I'd be writing about something else, but loading the bale dictates it has to lay on its round side with the center axis horizontal and aligned with the tailgate. So the trick is to get enough leverage against the truck cab and push with my legs to tip the bale so that it falls far enough to flip off the tailgate. The first time I did this it departed the vehicle as planned, and I made sure that our neighbors and the rest of the county were aware of my superhuman abilities. When you move a half ton by yourself, you have a deep desire to let people know via a primordial type of scream.

Not every unloading goes perfectly, and there is definitely an art to round bale handling. Still, with such a beautiful melding of technique, strength, and endurance training, I'm thinking about sharing my hay movement workout regimen. Now there's a business plan: provide an alternative for those who want workout options other than gyms. The membership fee would be relatively cheap; only a few carrots.

Four
Crazy from the Heat

Things have heated up in the loft recently, with this summer being one of the hottest and driest on record. The crunchy brown grass makes me wish that I had convinced my horse-loving honey to install some Grade A quality Brady Bunch Astroturf in parts of the yard. It would help with the mowing, too – once (if) the grass starts growing.

The horses have not enjoyed much the oppressive heat of the dog days of summer, and for that matter the dogs haven't looked too pleased either. Except our Jack Russell Terrier has discovered that he loves playing in a water bucket when he's out during the hot weather, so we leave one filled specifically for him.

Playing in water isn't limited to the dogs. Our percheron often paws (hoofs?) in the water trough. Yesterday I thought I finally felt some rain until I discovered the percheron, with his huge front feet, was sending jets of water into the air at near escape velocity.

If there's a silver lining to be found, it's that I haven't had to mow or bush hog recently. Silver linings do require clouds though.

The hot and dry conditions unfortunately have had an adverse effect on local hay production. When it gets to the point when you start looking at a wildflower wreath ornament in your bathroom as possible winter food for the ponies, something is wrong.

And I guess that really points to an interesting phenomenon. I do find myself thinking constantly as a responsible horse owner as opposed to a transplanted city dweller. Naturally, this has occurred slowly over nearly a decade, but when I look back at some events in my past, I certainly would see them in a different light today.

Many years prior to meeting she who would lead my indoctrination into all things equine, I was somewhat shocked one afternoon when I visited my girlfriend at the time at her house because of what I saw out the kitchen window. I asked her, who was not an equine-enamored person by any stretch of the imagination, if in fact I was looking at a horse in their back yard. Mind you, this house sat on a quarter-acre lot in a subdivision. Even to my young, untrained eye, a horse in such a place seemed out of place.

She confirmed it was indeed a horse (I had some equestrian knowledge back then I guess). I asked her what the horse was doing there, tied up at the fence with a lead line to its halter (although at the time I would have said something like rope and leather thingy). She replied, "He's just 'horse.' He likes it here."

OK, I'll admit, she wasn't the sharpest knife in the drawer. On further prying, I learned that the horse belonged to her cousin who had a mini-farm a couple miles away with some unplanned fence issues. So "horse" was temporarily staying attached to a fence in the backyard of her family's house in a typical

1970s era type subdivision while the fence was repaired.

Today, in addition to getting the nomenclature correct, I would immediately check to see if the horse had ample water and hay. Then I'd inquire if there was a paddock somewhere where it could walk about freely, preferably with a run in shed to protect from the direct sunlight and rain. But back then I simply shrugged my shoulders and took my girlfriend to see "Bill and Ted's Bogus Journey." That movie made more sense than the horse standing there.

Fast forward to now, and I find myself lucky to be with my equine-enamored counterpart who does have more sense than a roll of pennies. But I am concerned about the hot, dry weather effects on horse care, to the point where I often now am asking my bride about plans for winter feeding should the drought produce a much lower hay yield this season. She assures me that there are several options. I think I may have a few to help, and, no, they do not include feeding random house décor to the ponies in February.

To me, it could be as simple as gathering up all of the crunchy grass, weaving it together into hay appropriate lengths, and utilizing old hay strings to manually create small bales. Ok, that really is a bad idea, since I can't braid.

But yard sales typically have everything you can imagine. Maybe I should scour all possible yard sales every Saturday for the rest of the season for straw hats. Then, come February, I can be the hero when I produce enough hats that have the equivalent amount of straw for three round bales. No, that's not a good idea either; the hats would hold less nutritional than fashion value.

I must be too crazy from all this heat. I'm working on installing a single container beverage cooler on the mower for when I have to return to cutting the fields in the heat to avoid these and similar delusions. Last time I mowed in the heat, I thought I saw "horse" tied to a fence at a neighbor's house across the street. Bogus!

Five
Dog and Pony Show

Growing up in an urban apartment complex did not provide much opportunity to experience anything related to country living. Actually, where we lived could have been considered "the country," from a city dweller's point of view. The closest deli was at least three blocks away. My cousin had a big dog as they had the space for such – he lived further out in the country (five blocks from a deli).

In the small confined space of apartments, pet choices were limited to small dogs, cats, and fish. Although we once unexpectedly expanded the list when my siblings and I found a stick with what looked like a bubble in the bark and brought it inside. Shortly thereafter, on April Fools' Day no less, dozens of little praying mantises scattered from the egg to all four corners of their world (the living room). We successfully got all the new mantises outside to their natural habitat before our two cats ate any. We only had cats while I was growing up, no dogs (or fish for that matter).

What does any of this have to do with horses? Well, it seems like many equine lovers also love canines. Therefore, my first real exposure to the life of a dog was when I was engaged to my equine-loving girlfriend a few years earlier. The relationship was a package deal and the merger included her small pup and my two cats. A sort of mixed family menagerie, I guess.

This past fall, my canine-enamored cohabitant gave me two catalogues to pick out Christmas gifts, one for tack and one for dog accessories. You see, we have a simple Christmas tradition: she gives me a "tack wish list," and I suggest pilot accessories for me. Works out well in that we give each other what the other wants without much guesswork, and I get to avoid those uneasy Victoria's Secret visits.

She frequently hosts horseback riding lessons at our property with two or three friends, as we have a large front yard with jumps, some of which I constructed. Last summer, one of the riders brought a Jack Russell Terrier to the lessons, and my wife became attached to the dog. As it turns out, he became a "grand dog" in the fall, and the owner was looking for homes for the puppies.

With the catalogues came the choice: purchase tack or one of the pups along with associated puppy necessities (training crate, pen, squeaky toys, and pooper scoopers). I chose the latter, but have this nagging sense of guilt that the tack store balance sheets were significantly off this season without our order.

I have become quite comfortable purchasing tack. Whereas I couldn't tell a girth belt from a Garth Brooks a few years ago, now I know that "accepting the bit" does not always mean establishing a successful Internet connection. Switching gears to canine accessories would be tough, but ultimately I decided (much to my wife's pleasure) to purchase the pup and associated "puppy tack."

I have to admit, however, that I was worried about letting our new, young Jack Russell Terrier (Terrorist) around the horses. We also have a black Labrador Retriever, and he will never be mistaken for being undernourished, so his rather large frame is easily seen by the horses. But a Jack Russell Terrier never gets too big, maybe about the size of our cats (who also will never be mistaken for being underfed), and I was worried the horses wouldn't see him.

However, since his grandfather has been a frequent observer at the jumping lessons at our house, I am less concerned, as that one never put himself in danger from the ponies. Jack Russells, or at least the ones I've been exposed to, seem to be very well behaved, or maybe just quite smart. Something that small should know not to run under an animal that weighs almost a ton.

I do have a more serious concern. My wife has definitely bonded with our new arrival (as have I), and I'm afraid of the puppy distracting her as she rides. After all, it will soon be warm enough to begin outdoor lessons at our house again, and I know the pup will be out taking it all in. Fortunately, our lab has adopted to the role of big brother quite well, and will undoubtedly ensure "Little Bit" doesn't roam too far.

So in a couple of months it will be back to horses jumping obstacles at our household. The crew watching this equine and rider athleticism will increase by one, and any time a fan base increases, good things often happen. Now, if can just teach him how to operate a riding lawnmower . . .

Six
Let's Ride!

I do enjoy performing many of the farm chores, although in order to maximize my earning of sympathy points it is necessary, on occasion, to complain about them. There is a certain sense of tranquility that comes with cleaning stalls as the sun rises, and nothing tastes better than a cold Coke after tossing several dozen hay bales up to the loft. But if she who is my horse-loving partner knew I felt that way, I'd seriously jeopardize the not quite necessary but always welcome backrub to soothe the muscles strained while helping with the mini-farm's upkeep.

However, while one might say that the satisfaction is in the journey, and not the destination, ultimately as I dump the last load on the manure pile, I'm left to ponder that there must be more – not manure, rather more to experience from horse care and ownership. And of course there is. Whether it be simply trail riding, three-day eventing, fox hunting, or one of dozens of other horse-human activities, riding is both exhilarating and soothing.

Unlike a car, when a horse doesn't "work right" you cannot pull over, jiggle a few wires, yell "Honey, try it now," and hope that you have maintained proficiency in Wire Jiggle 101. No, "the ride" requires a unique understanding between horse and human. It is a partnership, and a beautiful one at that.

When it came time for my first experience at trail riding, I naturally figured the best way to approach the ride was to create the spirit of partnership with the pony. Horses weigh a lot, and are big and tall, whereas I weigh much less (well, more than I should, but blame that on chicken wings), and am small and short. My seven years spent obtaining a degree in engineering gave me the smarts to do the math. This four-legged wonder could make me look like Beetle Bailey after an encounter with Sarge, so I'd better make friends fast.

Carrots are a horse's best friend, so I tried to grow some in my garden for them. Lesson number one: scraping a half inch trench in hard clay, dumping in carrot seeds, and praying for rain doesn't yield anything but dead, dirty seeds. Fortunately, there is a Kroger with a great produce section nearby. My soon-to-be partner in the ride was quite appreciative at my yummy orange gift.

It is important for one's "first ride" that the horse be as docile and understanding as possible, sort of a Fred Rogers in the equestrian world. Fortunately, my first trail riding experience would be on one of the most forgiving and gentle horses, an appaloosa that my equestrian-loving eventual spouse had raised. This appy, while filled with kindness and not a mean bone in her body, possessed a smart and mischievous streak. I should have known that from the look she gave me as I fed her pre-ride treats, as if she was saying "I'll take care of you, but you're mine!"

It didn't help that some appaloosas, including her, have a bit more white in their eyes, which appears to accentuate the mischievous aspect of their personality when they look at you at an angle. Several times, as I learned about how to prep for the ride (saddle pad, saddle, girth, stirrups, reins, life insurance policy up to date), I swear she licked her lips in anticipation of "the newbie." Learning that there was no seat belt for the saddle did not ease my worries.

In all fairness, she took very good care of me on the first trail ride. Although I have no doubt that every time we came across a low branch on the trail she purposefully moved close enough to it so that I'd get whacked in the face.

Trail riding is fun, but I wanted to (and still want to) become a better rider. To me, that doesn't mean going faster or higher, but learning about how to work as a team with the horse. My wife, AKA my equestrian trainer, recognized this desire, and with a similar glint in her eye, suggested a session on the lunge line. Once I realized it wasn't some form of country dance, I agreed to it.

We did one "lunge session," and personally I was glad I didn't actually have to lunge at anything. I must have done ok because the next time my wife/trainer suggested we "sit the trot without stirrups." That means as much to me as "Fed increases interest rates to promote economic expansion," so I deferred to the expert (as all good husbands should).

I performed ok, which in my world means I didn't fall off, but my wife seemed pretty impressed that I was able to "sit the trot without stirrups" so early in my training, despite some sore muscles.

Naturally, I parlayed that into an extra-long backrub that night. I don't think she noticed though that I walked a bit different for the next day or so. If she did, she never said anything.

So today, I consider myself a newbie with some potential. At the very least, I am convinced that riding is not as easy as John Wayne, Bruce Davidson, or the Lone Ranger made it look. Certainly, the proper attire is extremely important . . . and I don't mean just for presentation purposes.

Seven
Fenced In!

In my childhood, I learned much about horse boarding from watching Bonanza. Horse care consisted of moving hay from place to place, fixing fences that seemed to break on their own, and letting horses drink from a wooden trough after a ride into town. Adam, Hoss, Little Joe, and Ben must have been very successful at raising and caring for horses and livestock, as they had a wonderful house situated on The Ponderosa, a land mass out west roughly the size of Connecticut.

When my horse-loving significant other informed me that we needed to add fencing to build a paddock off our barn for keeping our mare off of fescue while she was in the last stages of gestation, questions raced in my mind, from "Why can't the mare eat fescue?" to "What is the gestation period for a horse?" I was proud of the fact that I knew what fescue and a paddock were by this time; after all I had been a horse spouse for several years. I figured another learning session was around the corner.

My first encounter with fencing technology actually was when we had moved to the mini-farm, when I came to understand some technical terms such as brace post, woven wire, and hanging gates. Gate hanging sounds like a simple concept. However, as my equine education experience has revealed, nothing is simple. When we had cleared and prepared the front field for housing horses, the final step left to full functionality was to repair the gate between that and our back field.

A gate is a simple mechanical device, with relatively few moving parts: two hooks, one gate, and two hinges clamped on to the gate via bolts. My singular goal was to make the gate separating two fields more secure. The previous owners had hung the gate with both hinge pin hooks facing up, which, according to my equine-expert wife, could allow a horse to lift the gate off the hinges – clearly a safety issue defeating the gate's purpose. As I possess a mechanical engineering degree from a prestigious university, my professional analysis concurred with her assessment, and I went about designing a better mouse trap. In other words, I took her suggestion to turn one of the hinges downward, thereby "trapping" the gate.

After prepping the work area (drill, bore, gloves, pipe wrench, socket wrenches, box end wrenches, radio, and stocked cooler), I set about to remove the gate, reposition the hinge, and reinstall the gate, confident that I could finish the job before halftime of the Titans – Raiders game. About seven minutes remained in the second quarter with the Titans winning when I proudly finished tightening the second hinge clamp.

After a well-earned break, I tested the gate. Like a ballet dancer, the gate gracefully arched open. Midway through its perfect swing, a loud bang rang out and the gate began to drag. The repair had failed.

Gate hanging requires only one pivot point, but if the clamps holding the hinges in place are not tight enough, another pivot point between the gate and the clamp emerges and ends up becoming the dominant one. The movement caused the clamps to loosen, resulting in the gate tipping downward and dragging on the ground.

I lost valuable time in my analysis to arrive at this conclusion. It was now the third quarter and the Titans were losing, but I had come up with a plan. Apparently, however, my approach needed more refining, as the Titans lost, and so did I. To put it bluntly, I could not fix the gate easily. A 30-minute project turned into hours, then days.

The following week, my significant other suggested that maybe we should call an expert. No way was I going to let a single pivot point collection of metal tubing get the best of me! No, by this point in time it was personal. Don't get me wrong, as there are several things I will defer to experts (a broken septic tank pump for example) but this was a gate. Besides, the "call an expert" line is akin to laying down a challenge. I was dared to fix it, and I had better do so not only correctly but in a timely fashion. Once the "expert" option is mentioned, it's notification that the game was almost up, so I had to switch to two-minute drill mode.

I had the right size clamps and bolts; actually several of them as I went through three or four pairs trying to get the gate to work. I looked on the Internet for instruction on how to hang gates, but came away with nothing; apparently it is so simple that no one felt it worth writing about (until now, of course). All I had to do was to find some way to get those clamps to stop moving. No amount of tightening worked, but I thought I'd found a solution by using roof tar as glue. It almost worked, but a failure is a failure. Out of timeouts with the clock ticking, I had to punt.

With my sanity and reputation on the line, a wild idea formed in my head. I know my wife was quite worried when she saw me going to the gate armed with only a drill, hammer, and nails. But perseverance and gray matter finally won, as a couple of nails inserted into holes drilled through the clamps and then hammered down made a quite effective key to hold the clamps. After more than a week, I had solved the problem, not long before the end of the regular season.

Thus, when it came time to build the paddock, my horse-loving wife suggested we take up an offer from friends experienced in such construction to help, and I agreed without hesitation. I know she offered it in a manner to pacify me, by saying that we can both learn from our seasoned friends how to install T-posts, poles, and so on. I gladly played along and accepted the offer, saving face while relieving both of us of the worries of me trying to do it myself. Besides, if I built it at half the rate as I fixed the gate, the pony would be a full-grown mare when I finished it. But I bet I can now hang a gate better than all four of those Cartwrights combined.

Eight
Mow, Mow, Mow!

Our first house was essentially a starter home that sat on a half-acre lot in a suburban subdivision. The largest piece of land-working machinery we owned then was a Murry 3.5 horsepower push mower, and represented my only experience with mowing equipment. Prior to getting married, I lived in zero lot line condos and apartments in various places including Buffalo, NY, where there are only two seasons: "summer," from June 3rd to August 7th, and "snow," the rest of the year. Snow shoveling I excelled at, but I never really had an opportunity to learn much about mowing until owning the starter home.

There is nothing wrong with boarding horses, but my wife wanted the ponies to be as close to her as possible. A trot-up window at the house for carrot takeout orders was a primary goal of her mare (and still is). Thus, shortly after we married we found a house with a small barn and enough pasture to keep the horses with us and me busy.

The property featured a front yard large enough to host a football game. Mowing with the Murry was not a realistic option, though to say I dismissed the idea immediately would be a lie. I calculated though that if I tried use the push mower for front yard maintenance, I'd have to start back at the beginning as soon as I finished to keep the grass below knee level. It was time to purchase our first riding mower, a small green machine without a cup holder.

After a year or so of living on the mini-farm, I had come to understand the value of pastures that consisted primarily of grass with minimal weeds. For the more grass available for the horses to eat, the less hay I had to toss up, down, and all around – a huge incentive for me. To encourage grass growth and reduce the weeds, we would have the pastures bush hogged a couple of times a year. Each occurrence was not exactly cheap, but a tractor of our own to perform the work was out of our budget at the time. It was one fateful afternoon staring out into the pasture of weeds and grass, pondering the economics of cutting, when I uttered to myself four words that to this day I'm not sure was an expression of genius or an indication of severe frugality: "I can mow that."

Mowers in pastures are to rocks like backhoes are to underground utility lines and magnets are to nails – you get the idea. Thusly, after mowing part of one pasture for the first time, I learned how to change mower blades. I hit one rock so violently that the blade bent into the ground, changing the mower to a mutant cross between an auger and a tiller. Still, changing out mower blades proved easy even for me, and mowing the pastures did eventually have the desired effect of keeping the weeds at bay and allowing the grass to grow. The ponies were happy, my wife was happy, and even with the increased blade costs, relatively speaking my wallet was happy, too.

A side benefit of mowing was the low vantage point the ride offered for close-up scanning of the fields for locating rocks and sinkholes. We live in a part of the country where sinkholes and rocks are common, and both can be harmful to a horse (particularly if a hoof jams in a sinkhole). Enter brilliant idea numbers 343 and 344. I bolted a bucket onto the back of the riding mower for rock collection, and whenever I found a new small sinkhole, I'd empty the bucket's contents into it. The other idea was to bolt an insulated cup holder to the mower. Brilliant!

 Despite the fact I was riding a loud beast in their domain, the ponies generally ignored me as I puttered by. Occasionally, one or more would come near to offer to help or, more likely, see if Dad had some carrots in his overall pockets. Once, I found one nibbling on the cup holder when I returned from a break. I sensed they were happier with me riding the mower instead of them.

 In the course of learning about proper horse diet and pastures, I have become somewhat of an amateur mower mechanic. Not long ago, I purchased another riding mower at a garage sale for five dollars just to convert the tires and frame into a cart (the bucket for rocks wasn't as efficient as I'd hoped), but was able to repair it completely and now use it exclusively for cutting the fields.

 Eventually we will purchase a tractor, and I'll probably be able to rework one of these mowers into a tiller. I've saved enough warped blades already to spin down a variety of depths. Or maybe I'll just build an automated carrot delivery system for the ponies.

Nine
Training Wheels

Different stages of pursuits require different training methods until skills are acquired and mastered before advancing to the next level. Evel Knievel once used training wheels on his bicycle, I'm sure. It is the same with riding horses, although my wife nixed the idea of putting training wheels on our appaloosa for my first ride some years ago. As our goals change, so must our training methods.

At one time, my horse-hobby wife mentioned an interest in fox hunting. I didn't know much about it, beyond what I'd seen in Warner Brothers' cartoons as a child. I wasn't too thrilled with the idea, until I learned that the American version of fox hunting focuses on the chase and not killing a fox. The hunt ends when a fox enters a hole or the dogs lose the scent, so the foxes tend to shower well the morning of the hunt.

The idea of racing on horseback through woods following dogs instead of well-travelled paths just seems dangerous to me. I'm not sure how someone learns how to do this, as the training wheels would surely snap off after hitting the first protruding root, right? But I think my wife may still be interested in fox hunting, as I'm suspecting she's developed a method to train at home. Our resident fox couple on our property is now the proud parents of five pups (which I named Larry, Curley, Moe, Curley

Joe, and Shemp), and I think she has worked out some sort of training deal with the foxes in exchange for free room and board.

Of course, whether fox hunting, rodeo riding, or joining a posse with Matt Dillon and Festus, the horse is a necessary piece of equipment for successful rides, so choosing the right one for the job is important. Sometimes it helps if the horse's attributes match the rider's to an extent. For example, if I ever get into cross-country riding, my horse would stand at the start line for a minute or so then run the course like a madman (mad horse?) to get done in the desired time. Did I forget to mention I'm a procrastinator? I'll get around to it.

Eventually the time came for my significant other to look for a new training partner (horse) in order to reach the next skill level. This would involve relocating the current training partner, as we prefer to maintain a three-horse operation. Finding a suitable home is not as easy as it may seem, as it is very important to both of us that any horse we sell will be treated well, have plenty of room to exercise, be worked (everyone needs a purpose), and have an unlimited carrot expense account.

After several weeks and some test drives (rides), she settled on a percheron thoroughbred cross. "Percheron" sounded to me like something that a bird does, so my equestrian-expert attempted to educate me. "He's part draft, with feet the size of small pizzas." See, my wife knows how to explain things to me – break any complex issue down into beer and food components or analogies and I get it every time.

Within a week, our newest addition to the herd had arrived. The feet were in fact the size of personal pan pizzas. I just hope our farrier doesn't charge by the inch. This horse was definitely built like a Clydesdale, albeit much smaller. I knew what a Clydesdale looked like from watching Budweiser commercials during Yankees games growing up, making me a self-proclaimed expert on draft recognition. Since draft horses are bred for work, I began pondering the possibility of strapping a finishing mower to a harness.

Our landscape has changed a bit, and as my wife begins to bond with her new draft training partner and the fox pups are growing and leaving the den more often. I can tell they're about ready to strike out in the world on their own, as yesterday I noticed a pile of small training wheels discarded by the den entrance.

Ten
Hay!

Summer's arrival brings the enjoyment of fine traditions representative of the warm season. There's nothing like sipping lemonade under a large shade tree while taking a break from yard work, eating a hot dog at a baseball game, or watching nature unfold before your eyes while tending to gardens and flowerbeds.

On the other end of the spectrum, there is the summer stocking of hay.

For those who have enough land to be completely self-sufficient in hay, cutting in the summer is a necessity, if only to keep fields from turning into woods. Baling is then a natural extension of cutting to avoid waste. I can relate, much to my wife's chagrin, as I find it difficult to throw things away. Yes, I can make something out of that old rusted tank heater. Something.

But for those who rely on the tried and true capitalist methods of acquiring hay for winter, it must be bought and stocked in the summer, much as squirrels hoard acorns. Initially I didn't understand why we needed to acquire hay in the summertime, as why would the horses need hay when they've got pastures of green grass to turn into manure to create more grass? Well, try buying hay in January.

The easiest and most common method for purchasing hay is to find a local hay farmer. Usually this isn't too hard to do; look for a freshly cut green field spotted with square or round bales. Don't be surprised to see a hand painted sign on any structure nearest to said field that says "Hay for Sale." Or you could drive with one friend of mine around the countryside. He about gave me a heart attack one day while driving when he suddenly shouted "HAY!" After I removed my foot from the new hole in the truck's floorboard and pulled the brake pedal back into the cab, he explained it was an inside (outside?) joke to shout "HAY!" when seeing bales of hay in a field. Ha!

Once a hay source has been located, the quality of the hay should be determined before purchasing. At bare minimum, the hay should not contain any tree limbs. It should not be moldy, identified when moving a bale results in the release of a small swarm of mold spores. It should be cured but not fossilized. Finally, it should not contain a live snake. Trust me.

My equestrian-loving wife found a supplier of quality hay not more than a couple of miles from our mini-farm not long after we moved there, and we routinely purchase from him a few times a year. That farmer has about the greenest thumb I've ever seen; in addition to quality hay, he grows vegetables and is a regular at the local farmer's market. I don't know his tricks, but in the spring his tomato plants are often already tall, bushy, with flowers and growing fruit, whereas mine resemble Charlie Brown's Christmas tree.

Many hay resellers store their hay in a barn, whereas some let you pick it up in the field for a reduced price right after baling during the growing season. Of course, this means another round of lifting and stacking hay in the hot summer sun, since you cannot bale wet hay (see mold comment above). There is an art to stacking hay in a truck and a flatbed trailer (especially when the truck is slowly moving through the field). You want to maximize the load carried while minimizing the chance of seeing hay bales in the road in the rear view mirror when driving home, all while ensuring truck or trailer tires do not run over your feet.

  I did enjoy our most recent field gathering experience, although once again I felt a sense of emptiness and envy. As we drove away, carefully watching to ensure we didn't lose any bales, I couldn't help but notice with envy the collection of machinery labeled Kubota, John Deere, and International. After I helped unload the hay at our barn, it was back to work riding the Murray 11 HP 38-inch cut.

Eleven
Blazing Trailers

Shortly before we married, my horse-enamored fiancé remarked one afternoon that earlier that day she had seen a fabulous trailer. The best trailer I could remember viewing was for Star Trek II in the early 80s. KHANNNNNNN! But somehow I got the feeling she wasn't referring to movie trailers.

She of course was talking about a horse trailer, and proceeded to gush about aspects she liked on the one she'd seen. Most of the features hovered above my brain, not quite processed, but they sounded expensive. She didn't realize back then that spouses of horse lovers need to hear the most important variable of proposals first: the cost.

Now, I understand the concept of inflation, but to purchase this rolling horse transport would require the expenditure of triple the greenbacks my parents spent on their first abode, a small house, in the days before color TV. I did try to see her point of view about the benefits of buying a quality trailer, and filed the information in the back of my mind as I responded casually "Well, we'll look at it after we get married." My fiancé's giddiness betrayed that her mind translated my words as "We *will get it* after we are married."

The time eventually came to look at buying a trailer. Personally, I figured if we're going to get a feature rich one, we should at least insist on large seats for the horses to sit down. Having grown up riding New York City subways, I was acutely aware of the unpleasantness of standing in an aluminum tube on a hot summer's day being transported somewhere. However, no trailers we looked at had such seats or even strap-hangers, not that a horse could actually grab a hanger for balance.

Actually, I have to admit, I was lost on the concept of needing a trailer to haul horses in the first place. Were not these magnificent creatures bred for transportation? Hello? I mean, I never saw John Wayne unload a horse from a trailer outside of town and then ride it to the saloon.

Well, she eventually found success in convincing me of a need for a trailer, but I was already thinking ahead. These things didn't exactly move by themselves, unless one gutted a Winnebago (not a bad idea, if you think about it). That not being an option, we'd need something to pull the trailer.

I knew this would be a problem. Early in our courtship, I, the "wanna-be outdoorsy" type driving a six cylinder Ford Ranger with a bumper hitch, offered to pull a trailer she had talked about borrowing. If the truck could pull a jet ski, surely it could haul a small horse trailer. She laughed and gently explained why it probably wasn't a good idea. Incidentally, when I did sell that truck several years later, the bumper wasn't exactly in its original configuration, but that's a story for another day.

My eyes glazed over with dollar signs and my wallet groaned only partially from me sitting on it as my lovely wife said we'd need to buy another truck. A big truck. A diesel truck that could accommodate a gooseneck. Now, I knew that diesel was that stuff that came out of the green hose at Shell, but I was initially lost on how geese fit into this equine transport plan.

Time marched on, and money is meant to be spent, and we did just that, purchasing a big diesel Ford and a trailer that was more spacious than my first apartment. The large aluminum equine transport had a big ramp on the back that came down like one on a military landing craft. I admit it made it easy to walk in and out of, which was a good thing because the horses would have a difficult time squeezing through the side door.

I guess the equine mind doesn't think the same as that of a horse-lover's spouse, as one of our horses didn't find the idea of walking on the ramp a particularly pleasant one. In the span of only a few minutes, I learned that trailer loading is not an instinctive activity for a horse. That's why George Washington crossed the Delaware River in a rowboat; he couldn't load his horse on the landing craft.

I also learned you can't bribe, coax, reason with, or push a horse up that ramp. Trying to load a horse on a trailer when the horse is convinced the trailer is going to eat him really is like pounding a square peg into a round hole. This frustrated my wife as well, and she wasn't too amused when I suggested that perhaps the horse simply wanted to drive.

Eventually, of course, the horse did load, and off he and my wife went to a riding lesson. As I watched them pull away, I remembered my subway days, and thought the horse would be bored during the trip. I didn't even give him a newspaper to read – how thoughtless of me. I began to think about installing a TV and a VCR to keep the ponies occupied on their journey, and went into the house to look for my old VHS copy of Star Trek II.

Twelve
Crossing Bridges

One of my early mini-farm projects was to replace the "bridge" that spanned our seasonal runoff creek. The structure really wasn't a bridge, rather a small boat dock that at one time functioned as a crossing but had deteriorated with many rotted areas, clearly a potential horse hazard. While our land doesn't exactly drain well, I couldn't figure out how a dock floated to that location. I hoped it was placed there intentionally.

Bridges connect things, be it two sections of land, verses in songs, or even teeth. Even time can be considered a bridge between events, such as twelve months ago and today. Then, I had gotten the call every horse loving spouse dreads, and in short order I was in the emergency room with my wife, her foot not quite positioned the way it was supposed to be. Whatever she does, she does well, and a bone fracture was no exception. She still has enough metal in her ankle to make her cringe going through airport security.

While she occasionally expressed apprehensions about getting back on a horse, she knew that the fall from her pony was a fluke, and that she would ride again. So, during her recovery period, I spent much time working to increase the safety on the mini-farm. I learned many things, some actually useful.

For example, used racquetballs make excellent stall latch guards. The only problem is playful ponies see the colorful orb as either a toy or a challenge. I found myself replacing these racquetball latch covers rather frequently. I play enough racquetball though to have an ample supply of dead balls.

I was quite proud of myself when I installed a homemade cup holder on my little red ancient riding mower. In short order, however, I discovered my imaginative accessory did not work well for carbonated beverages. The mower's shaking and jostling, especially after hitting a rock, flattens the drink faster than a semi hitting a squirrel. But non-carbonated beverages such as lemonade and iced tea handled the rough ride well, so I still ended in the plus column on this one.

Sinkholes are common in our area. Fortunately though, they are not the humongous variety that can swallow cars and elephants, rather they are more like glorified mole holes. I remember once our little terrier mix, quite old and nearly blind, was eagerly jogging in the yard towards me when suddenly she vanished from sight. I didn't have time to panic, as almost immediately her little head popped up from a hole in the grass with a confused look. To ensure small pets and legs do not suddenly disappear in a similar manner, I now always keep a bag of Quikrete quick setting concrete mix on hand for not only projects such as resetting poles but also for filling sink holes. If you opt to use the 90-pound bag, keep your health insurance current to handle the inevitable hernia operation expense.

Manure piles generate heat – I never knew that. I ran for the barn fire extinguisher one morning when I saw what looked like smoke signals rising from "Mount Manure." It turned out that what I had observed was steam from heat produced by the composting of the waste. I now agree with my wife's assertion that we need a manure spreader. I used to think I was enough.

On that subject, horses produce manure . . . a lot. Honestly, though, I've not only become quite good at cleaning stalls, I actually like it. And that disturbs me. It's therapeutic in an odd sort of way.

Trees fall in the worst possible direction. My wife must possess some measure of ESP, as not long after she bought me a chain saw for Christmas, four of the Bradford Pear trees lining our driveway gave in to the dark side of the wind, each fallen trunk blocking vehicular access. Still, I enjoyed cutting them. Every time I wield the chain saw I feel like Ash from "Army of Darkness." "Alright, who wants some?"

Horses are not dogs. They do not come when you call them (well, usually). Therefore, always have some carrots on hand. A carrot in hand is worth three horses in the barn.

No matter how many times I've done it, I'm still surprised at the (should be expected) shock whenever I absent-mindedly clutch the electric fence. I think I may have a bit of Bart Simpson in me. "Ow! Quit it. Ow! Quit it. Ow! Quit it."

But building the bridge was quite a learning experience in itself. There are tons of bridge building resources available on the Internet, and I utilized none of them. I recalled my college engineering education, sharpened my slide rule, adjusted my pencil, and designed a bridge that was strong enough to support a horse and wide enough for a mower to cross. Of course, building that bridge provided an easy access to our back field, allowing for more frequent mows – so maybe I'm not as smart as I think I am.

Today my wife looks wonderful back in her element, galloping and jumping, well past the other end of her recovery bridge. As for my bridge, last week, as I was walking back up our long driveway, morning newspaper in hand, I looked towards the back field and saw not one but two horses standing on the bridge, with a fresh mound of steaming manure in the middle between them.

Thirteen
Test Out!

We encounter tests constantly in all facets of life, including while performing the duties of horse-lover's spouse. Those trials are not of the traditional paper and guess variety, of course. Instead of a grade, results may range from a successful ride (in other words, I didn't fall off) to a barn boot with an arc indent over the toes from not watching where a pony was stepping. And I thought that F I received in tenth grade geometry was painful!

Early in our courtship, I learned how to quickly and efficiently earn a substantial amount of brownie points with her. All I had to do was accompany my equine-educator to a horse show as "horse show helper." The first competition I assisted at started very early on a Saturday, and I assumed (incorrectly) such would mean an early completion and leave us with plenty of time to drive home and catch the Tennessee – Florida game on TV. As time ticked down to kickoff, the activities at the horse event went on, and I grew increasingly fidgety. Fortunately, my then future wife was (and still is) a college football fan as well, and she deducted no brownie points when I disappeared to the cab of the truck to listen to the game on the radio.

Sometimes I am not able to make horse shows because of duties around the mini-farm creating scheduling conflicts. This seems to be particularly true starting in early September. Mowing the yard and fields takes much time, and to alleviate the boredom I listen to a radio, earbuds under my hearing protectors. I divide the yard and fields into three jobs: "Vols," "Blue Raiders," and "Titans." Touchdown!

Horse shows are of course themselves tests, competitions that evaluate preparation, skill, and mental toughness. A cross-country course tests my equine-enamored partner's resolve and my queasiness. I cringe every time my wife seemingly forgets that horses do not in fact have wings.

Of course, I'm not the only one constantly tested while engaging in equine care activities. A few days back I caught a glimpse through our living room window of my appaloosa aficionado running across the front yard, from barn to front field gate. She was actually in a race with our cunning appy (who was racing across the back fields) to reach the front field first. We've been letting that field grow, therefore the grass there is thick and lush, the horse dinner equivalent to a 20-ounce New York strip steak. But too much of a good thing makes for a rounder appy, so we limit the horse's grazing times in that field. My wife won that test, and she was so fast that I entered her in a 5K race the next weekend.

A horse-lover's spouses' patience is sometimes tested. Mind you, these tests of patience are not as bad as being in the "15 Items Or Less" line behind someone with 22 items (everyone counts, it's ok to admit it). No, horses test patience with carefully designed team plays. One will wait and sneak into a paddock or a stall when another has just been led out.

Then, for some reason, the horse remains in the "forbidden zone," convinced that the paddock grass is greener or that their buddy left some feed in their stall bucket (never, ever happens). While I formerly used a lead rope to solve these problems, I've gotten smarter and have mounted a small TV/DVD combination player in the run in shed with a five episode "Mr. Ed" DVD in constant rotation. A horse is a horse, of course, of courses, and a horse cannot ignore Mr. Ed, of course . . .

Of course, I also tend to test my equine educator's patience, probably more so than she lets on. She had a disapproving tone in her voice during a recent phone conversation when she asked if I had remembered to chock the trailer after unhooking it from the truck. I have an engineering degree and a decent grasp of gravity, yet I'm still surprised when she informs me that the trailer has mysteriously rolled into a small sinkhole or up against the tree because of a missing small triangular piece of wood from under the wheels.

Sometimes I even test my own patience. I still am embarrassed that it took the better part of last football season (or so it seemed) to successfully hang a single gate. Perseverance eventually won out on that project, but only because I was allowed to retake that test several dozen times.

Unlike traditional education, which usually terminates with a diploma, degree, or certificate, the education and testing of a horse lover's spouse is an ongoing journey. These days, I tend to do better on those tests, though, now that I've been bringing my four-legged instructors apples on a regular basis.

Fourteen
Horse Flies

Learning about horses has been challenging, particularly as my only relevant childhood equine experience was riding an ancient carousel at an amusement park outside of New York City. However, my wife was not the only one who brought a steep learning curve hobby to our relationship. I have my pilot's license and enjoy flying my single engine Cessna 172. Actually, I've been amazed at how many aviation/equestrian relationships I have encountered. We have several horse loving friends whose spouses are pilots, and vice versa. I don't know what that implies, but someone in academia should write a paper on it.

If she explains horse concepts in flying terms, I can understand them better. However, shared nomenclature can lead to outright confusion. An airplane's wings will "stall," or not provide lift, when the airflow over the wing is not sufficient. Horses hang out in stalls, but a plane will never stall in a hanger. The words are the same but the definitions do not match. Why do people drive on parkways and park in driveways?

Both flying and riding disciplines require preparation and a slight, gentle touch. Pulling back too rapidly on an airplane's control wheel can cause the aircraft to stall, flip, spin, and race for the ground in a most unnatural manner. While I've never seen a horse stall, flip, and spin with too much pulling on the reins, that's a good thing, as in an airplane you usually have a few thousand feet to recover as opposed to a dozen or so hands.

That leads to another point of confusion shared by aviation and equestrian – the application of terminology unique to the environment. I'd like to know the first person who measured a horse by hands, and whether a smaller hand guy like me would make a fortune trading horses. I'd guess 14 "Herman Munster" hands horse equals about two dozen of my hands.

Aviation does borrow equestrian terminology, at least in measuring engine performance. Airplane engine power output is measured in "horsepower." My Cessna has a 150 horsepower engine, but there is a 160 horsepower version available. Sometimes I ponder where I can get ten more horses to go faster. I suppose I could hitch ten horses to the front, but then I'd be risking a lawsuit by infringing on the Santa Clause "Sleighmaster 3000" patent.

Slipping an airplane is a useful maneuver to land in crosswinds and to lose altitude in a rapid yet controlled manner. Slipping a horse is an uncontrolled maneuver, and may result in a busted fence (or worse).

It should be obvious by now that trying to equate riding concepts with flying is not as quite as simple as I'd hoped. The first time I found my steed going too fast while trail riding I tried to deploy the flaps to reduce my airspeed. We never did find that saddle pad.

But there are many similarities, such as weekend fly-ins and riding events. You travel to the gathering, meet others who share the hobby, exchange stories, eat food, and go home. I see an opportunity to combine the two but have been having a heck of a time trying to add a trailer hitch to the airplane. Actually, that's probably not possible, as flying is governed by pretty strict laws. I'm not talking the Federal Aviation Administration regulations; I'm referring to the laws of physics.

My wife would definitely make a good pilot. She has actually expressed an interest in learning to fly, and has done well navigating and landing Air Force One on the Las Vegas strip using Microsoft Flight Simulator. However, I'm pretty sure she gets enough altitude experience just directing her horse over stadium and cross country jumps. Me, I wouldn't try that unless the horse was properly equipped with an altimeter (and me with a parachute).

But we are able to combine our hobbies occasionally. Often while she is out riding in our practice field, I'll be circling overhead in the Cessna, and we'll wave to each other. And, inevitably, when we're traveling, we subconsciously fall back into our favorite hobbies. When driving, we both often find ourselves slightly pulling back on the steering wheel when approaching a hill. For me, it's a yoke to clear an obstacle on takeoff; her, reins in preparation to fly over a jump. Yee hah!

Fifteen
Wooden it be Nice

Our barn, like most, is made of wood. I think its primary component is oak, but when we first moved here, you could have told me it was bamboo and I would not have known the difference. Growing up in the city, my lumber construction experience was limited to a 200 piece "Lincoln Log" set.

The barn features a classic design and even has a birthing stall (which would come in handy later). Yet shortly after moving to the mini-farm, we realized we needed to add some features to enhance functionality. The first modification was at the request of my equestrian-enamored wife. She wanted a bar across the barn doors. This request excited me, and I began to research bar stools, the best beer taps, and dartboard selections when she informed me she simply meant a wooden bar to keep the horses in the barn hallway when the main doors were open. Cheers!

The bar she wanted seemed like a simple project to construct and install. I went about designing a slot on either side of the doors to slide a twelve-foot two-by-six into. These receivers consisted of two pieces of two-by-two, cut to about six inches, mounted on the sides of the wall, with a bottom brace. Implementation of this ingenious design taught me that oak is hard to nail into, small pieces of wood split, and bent nails are painful (particularly fingernails).

Eventually, after a few failed starts, I completed the project. The horses could hang out in the hallway without the fear of them deciding to do a walkabout to the front road. That is, until our younger pony decided to run through the barn while the bar was in place. The two-by-six snapped, which is better than the horse injuring itself. Yeah, I designed it that way.

Replacing the bar was easy enough; purchase another two-by-six and cut it to the same length. After the third time a bar was broken, this time by our baby mare doing her best Pete Rose dive into third base, I grew a brain and bought several two-by-six beams at once. Naturally, one of the horses decided next to break part of the paddock fence instead.

Some wood can be an outright safety hazard. Such was the case when a tree over our runoff creek decided to give into gravity, lying across the major equestrian expressway between "back field" and "pole barn field." After configuring a detour, I cleared the tree, leaving the branches to the side, thereby implementing phase two: procrastination.

Honestly, I planned to haul the branches to the burn pile the next day, but my horse helpers had other ideas. Apparently the leaves of this tree were quite tasty, as all three ponies were over the leafy appendages like flies on, well, you know. While I didn't know what kind of tree this was, the horses loved it, and if I played my cards right, they'd have all the leaves off within a day or two, dropping the weight of the branches and thereby reducing my workload.

Well, I was luckier than Kenny Rogers drawing to an inside straight, as my four-legged friends not only ate all of the leaves, but began eating the bark as well. I figure another two weeks and the pile of branches will be a distant memory. I am a firm believer that procrastination is a valid strategy to accomplish jobs, whereas my wife simply calls me lazy.

She also decided that the large trunk of the fallen tree would make an excellent cross-country jump. When I asked her how she thought I'd move it to where she wanted it, she said that she had faith that I'd figure something out. So far, I'm leaning towards a solution involving a four-wheel drive vehicle and chains. If I can somehow work football and flying into the project it'll be perfect!

But I do realize that my wood clearing and carpentry skills need some work, particularly the latter. It's pretty evident that, sooner than later, we'll have to do some major barn siding repair work. To prepare for this, I have been learning about construction on a much smaller scale by building an addition to Man's World (my wife's term for my work shed). Actually, if I hadn't sold this project as a precursor to the barn work, I don't know if she would have readily agreed to it, which is yet again an excellent proof of horse-lover's spouse rule #4: you have a much better chance of getting what you want if you can show that it also benefits the horses. Unfortunately, my wife realizes horses cannot drive Corvettes.

While I work constructing Man's World Annex, I find myself contemplating adding a major flaw. It could cause my wife to hesitate and reevaluate my carpentry skills when barn repair time comes around, allowing me time to procrastinate further. That "wood" have been a good idea if I hadn't just exposed my plans by writing about it.

Sixteen
Cold Case

In retrospect, I wish I had benefitted from a guide to what every horse-lover's spouse needs to know regarding horse care in the winter. Therefore, this month's column is my gift to all of you who are experiencing the joys of helping with the horse chores when the temperature has fallen below freezing for the first time. The first rule is to always heed your partner's words of wisdom. When in doubt, reference this rule.

Horses need water in the winter, not ice cubes. Unless you're fortunate enough to have a tank heater, water in troughs will freeze. Tank heaters are not too expensive, but without a one, you'll need another piece of specialized equipment, albeit less sophisticated. It's called a hammer, and it doesn't cost much, unless it is listed as a "Solid Dihydrogen Monoxide Pulverizer."

Hammers do not come with instructions for how to bust ice in a trough, and for good reason. A hammer is not designed to break ice. While either end can be an effective striker for causing fissures in trough ice, often dangerous projectiles will scatter in random directions as a result of the strikes on the ice. I bought the companion to the Solid Dihydrogen Monoxide Pulverizer called Safety Glasses after a particularly large chunk of high velocity frozen water contacted my face, creating quite a shiner. Obviously, a tank heater's return on investment is in time saved splitting ice, not to mention cost savings from the otherwise inevitable doctor bills.

Of course, troughs cannot fill themselves, or at least I haven't figured out a way to accomplish that (although I'm still working on it). When we moved to our current place, we ran a water line to our barn, complete with one of those "will not freeze" faucets. When shut off, water drains down the pipe below the frost line (assuming the faucet's feed was properly installed below the frost line), preventing frozen pipes (and brains). In the event that the faucet does not work properly, often because of a broken seal, the best method to unfreeze the faucet is to pour hot water on it. Blowtorches are not a good idea, and that's all I want to say about that.

My horse-loving partner explained the proper multi-step process for filling a trough in winter is as follows:

    1) connect one end of hose to faucet
    2) drop other end in trough
    3) turn on faucet
    4) turn off faucet when trough is full
    5) disconnect hose
    6) drain hose by raising it above your head, walking the length of the hose, then walking the hose the other way
    7) hang hose on hose holder.

Thus, the first time I filled a trough in freezing weather, I connected the hose, filled the trough, turned off the faucet, and left the hose connected to faucet laying on ground. I have a degree in Mechanical Engineering; I know how to fill a trough.

Two days later, the trough needed refilling, and I increased the efficiency of the operation by skipping a couple of frivolous steps. I put the end of the hose in the trough, turned on the faucet, and proceeded to read the sports page. After finishing sports and the comics (the normal time required to fill a standard size trough), I went to check the water level of the trough.

I was madder than Superman on a kryptonite commode when I found the trough no fuller than it was when I started. No water was coming out of the hose. I accidentally stepped on the hose, and it crunched. I bent the hose a bit and a small cylindrical chunk of ice exited the end. No water was going through the hose while it was frozen. As I said in the beginning, remember rule #1.

No problem, I thought, as the sun was out and the air temperature had warmed to a balmy 35 degrees. The horses still had more than enough water, and a half hour out in the sun would melt the ice in the hose. I dragged my green snaking new nemesis out from the shadow of the barn and into the bright sunlight. Two hours later, the temperature had risen two degrees. Two more cylindrical pieces of ice had emerged from the hose on their own, but the majority of the water contained within remained solid. My wife was scheduled to come back from a horse show within the hour, so desperate measures were needed. Never give up, never surrender!

I ran inside, grabbed a hair dryer and a long extension cord, and set that Vidal Sasson on "Thermonuclear Obliterate." I paced that hose with the dryer like a curling sweeper cleaning the ice for the rock. Twenty minutes and a strained lower back later, I turned on the faucet and four cylindrical pieces of ice emerged. While my production had doubled, the clock was ticking, and I should have used a football analogy instead of a curling one.

There was a foolproof method to melt the remaining hose ice, and there was no bigger fool than I. I took the hose into the house and laid it on the tile floor of the mud room. With an ambient temperature of 71 degrees, I reasoned the ice should melt relatively fast, and it did. A nice puddle of melted hose water pooled in front of the washing machine. All part of my brilliant plan!

After hooking the hose back up, filling the trough, disconnecting and draining the hose (twice), and coiling it on the hose holder, I hustled to Man's World and retrieved a set of box wrenches, two vice grips, and a screwdriver, and moved the washing machine out from the wall. I heard the door open and saw a pair of britches, and mumbled that the washing machine had sprung a leak. As she exited to tend to the ponies, I breathed a sigh of relief. I needed a drink more than the horses did, and I would never forget rule #1 again.

Seventeen
All Wet

Horses are exposed to the elements constantly because horses spend much of their time outdoors – simple logic. While trees can provide some protection from the elements, often the horse owner must intervene to provide proper shelter from the sun and weather.

For example, we once had a paint gelding with a big, pink nose that had the tendency to easily sunburn. In the summer, the resident equine-expert had started this pony on a bi-daily regimen of sunblock to counter the sun's rays. Here was this manly horse, already suffering through adulthood without some of his manliness, forced to wear perfumed cream from a pink bottle. With no effort to hide his resentment, he would step on that bottle of sweet-smelling SPF 45 goodness with a manly gelding hoof whenever given the opportunity. When that was not possible, he would often try to hide it in his feed bucket.

A little display of rebellion goes a long way to restoring a sense of manhood, I guess. But guys, if you opt to try some James Dean inspired rebellion at home, don't blame me for the consequences. Incidentally, eating Jimmy Dean sausages is also quite manly.

Our appaloosa mare loves to stand outside in the rain. The harder and colder the falling water, the more she seems to enjoy it. Before we bought the mini-farm, we boarded the mare at a facility without a "run-in shed." Apparently such lack of basic amenities not only lowered this lodge's travel rating, it necessitated multiple trips to the barn for stall cleaning during periods of inclement weather as the mare spent more time indoors "doing her business."

However, because pride prevented me from displaying my ignorance by asking what a "run-in shed" was, I was left to my own devices to discern what she meant. "Why would a horse want to run into a shed?" I pondered. "Wouldn't that hurt? Was the shed padded?" Well, I found out my answer during a road trip when she pointed to a structure and indicated that was like the run-in shed we should have. Once again, procrastination produces results!

In fact, one reason we bought the mini-farm was the barn itself had one side configured as a shelter where all the horses could "run in" out of the rain. Well, most, as our appy still tends to ignore the shelter, preferring to bask in the summer's wetness.

When I moved to the south many moons ago, I kept hearing from the locals "If you don't like the weather, don't worry, wait a day and it'll change." Such cannot be said about my previous home city, Buffalo, New York, where an equivalent saying might be "If you don't like snow, cry." Still, here much of the weather comes in spurts, with days of sunshine followed by days of rain. Our property does not drain well in places, and a heavy rain can produce new lakes, wetlands, mud, and animals lining up in pairs.

To illustrate, last January we had a week of beautiful mild sunny weather, which of course meant the yang to that yin hit the following week with seven days of cold rain. The equine-loving better half decided that the next round bale we were to procure would go in the run-in shed side of the barn, since the field had become a mud pit. I had grave doubts about the ability to maneuver the round bale into such a confined space, but I positioned the truck just right to ensure a smooth push off and the round bale dropped perfectly below the overhang.

Moving the truck after delivery completion proved to be much more difficult, however. The mud suctioned the tires of our F-250. Every attempt to break free sank the vehicle a bit more. I am still embarrassed when I think of the ensuing conversation with the AAA tow truck driver:

"Doesn't your truck have four wheel drive?"

"Yes, sir," I replied, sheepishly.

"Wow. It takes a special kind of . . . person to get one of those stuck."

While in this case the round bale dropped perfectly into position, those large rolls of hay can usually be quite difficult to move. Despite their shape, they do not roll well. One time, my hay-expert wife determined a recently procured round bale was not fit for equine consumption (mold), her revelation occurring after we had unloaded it off the truck and cut the hay strings. We did not own a tractor (yet), so any maneuvering would have to be manual. We managed to roll the round bale out a gate about sixty years away, out of pony reach. Granted, the roll got easier as we progressed since the thing unraveled like a red carpet at the Oscars.

Back to the hay deposited in the run-in side of the barn. Now that dry food was available, all ponies, including the appy, converged under the shelter and commenced munching. While initially I had reservations about placing the bale in the confined space of the run-in, I will concede that if we had put it in the field it likely would have floated away by now. The ponies will whittle that bale down in short order, so we began to plan for the next round bale. The forecast is for five straight sunny days starting tomorrow, which means it will continue to rain.

Nope . . . I may be all wet, but the next time a tow truck comes to our address to remove the stuck F-250 from outside the run-in shed, I'll be hiding in the barn. I'll let the appy direct the towing as she stands in the glorious rain.

Eighteen
Horse Invasion

A few weeks ago, I received an after-hours emergency call from work to reboot a computer server at a time early in the morning when, in my college years, I'd just be getting to sleep. For the majority of my life, I have been a morning person, even in college, although back then my body seemed more adapted to Hawaiian time. However, four AM is just a bit early no matter what.

I am a radio talk show fan, but was not knowledgeable of the programs that were on that early. While driving to the office to restore all things Internet, I scanned the stations until something caught my ear – a caller discussing his previous life as a horse. I had to listen, if only to get material for this month's column. The caller explained how horses sometimes come back to life as humans to learn about human ways. They would then take this knowledge back to the horse collective consciousness. The caller went on to explain that, while he enjoyed walking upright, he yearned for the day when he could once again wear metal shoes. I'm serious – even I could not make this up!

I wish I could have listened further, but at about this time had I arrived at my destination, filled with thoughts of what the horse collective was trying to learn and I had to do my duty to satisfy someone who desperately needed to access the Internet at that crazy hour. I could not help but continue to ponder the caller's words as the server sprung to life. Could it be some sort of spy mission in preparation for a horse invasion? Like I said, I wish I could have listened to the radio show longer but that was all I had "herd."

Perhaps the horse collective wants an equine in the White House. Can it be just a coincidence that the symbol of the Democratic Party is equine? I can see the campaign slogan, modified slightly from Herbert Hoover's 1928 campaign: "A carrot in every feed bucket and a bale of hay in every stall!"

Of course, horses have historically positioned themselves close to great military leaders, often elevating them. From Caesar to Theodore Roosevelt, a horse was present, listening to every word of military secrets. I made a mental note to check paintings and pictures of historical figures on their steeds to see if the horses' ears were turned back or not. Perhaps, with the invention of the internal combustion engine and the vehicles that followed, horses, no longer granted favorable position in the tightest of military circles, devised the plan of walking upright to be close to the great military leaders as jeep (or today Humvee) drivers. You'd think it'd be easier just to come back as flies on walls. But then again, there are horse flies . . . hmmmm.

No, the intelligence-gathering angle just seems too absurd. It may simply be that horses are football fans, and until stadiums have club level stalls, reincarnation as a human is the only way a horse could attend a game. Certainly, Budweiser has picked up on this theory, as evidenced by their short documentaries of horses playing football in the snow (they are real, right?).

How could one tell if a person is really a horse? I think Robert Redford played just such a character in "The Horse Whisperer." What was he whispering to the horse in the scene where he was able to calm an unbroken horse? Frame by frame digital enhancement may have revealed the stunning truth. While quite grainy, Redford's lips seem to form these words: "So you went for two and missed. Get over it."

I don't think I was a horse in a previous life, but how can I be sure? When I was younger, my older brothers used to call me "Horse." So if I was "earlier equine," and I return to the horse collective, what would I tell them? I think the burden of tax season is beginning to wear thin on me, and since horses don't pay taxes, my only recourse would be to say, "Stay the course, be a horse!" In fact, I think I'd like to apply to be a horse, but if I did I'd try to deduct myself.

Horses could be looking for stardom. You'd think it'd be crazy to think that a horse would want to be on "American Idol," but consider that, in 1962, that TVLand icon, Mr. Ed, released the song "Pretty Little Filly." No, I don't think Mr. Ed would win Simon Cowell's praises.

Maybe I'm really over thinking this. Could it be that horses are just looking for a different diet besides grain, grass, hay, oats, carrots, and apples? Perhaps we can stop this horse invasion by simply ordering pepperoni pizzas for our ponies.

I guess we'll never know. But, after agonizing hours of analysis, my conclusion is that while horses may want to eat a brat at the stadium watching the Buffalo Bills, they should remain horses. And I need to stop listening to late night AM radio.

Nineteen
Spring Fling

There's nothing quite like spring. Beginning with March Madness and extending through Opening Day, the air is filled with the sounds of the crack of a bat, the smells of outdoor grilling, and the signs of life awakening from winter's nap all around. Not everything emerges at the same pace, and for some reason flies always seem to grab the pole position in the spring race.

As my wonderful equine-loving partner has hammered into my brain time and time again, piles of horse poop near the barn are bad not only because they attract said flies like shoppers to a blue light special, they're also not the healthiest thing for horses to step in, or two legged creatures, for that matter. We try to clean up these piles as often as possible, but sometimes we have unsolicited help.

Two of our dogs, both varieties of retrievers, love to eat horse dung. I cannot for the life of me figure out what is appealing enough about a pile of digested hay to generate thoughts of snacking. But both of them, particularly the golden retriever, look at these horse hockey puck piles like it's two for one buffet night at Shoney's. If that wasn't bad enough, their taste in droppings isn't limited to the equine variety. Contrary to Dogbert's self-proclaimed mission, dogs will never rule the world so long as they munch on cat doo.

Cleaning up horse poop really isn't that bad, especially if it's more than an hour old, as by that time the odor has greatly diminished. Based on extensive experience in such matters, I consider myself an expert in horse doo analysis and removal. Our youngest pony turns two this month, and while my wife measures her growth by what looks like a long T-square, from cleaning stalls and the barn perimeter I've seen the growth progress from marbles, to golf balls, to racquetballs, to tennis balls. If they reach bowling ball size, I'm quitting.

There must be an official name for the measuring apparatus, but "T-square thingy" works fine here. My percheron-parading partner (I'm running dry on horse-related wife descriptions, obviously) has remarked that the youngest grows in uneven spurts, with her hind currently higher than her withers. I guess she knows this because the hind-wither line is not at a right angle to the vertical as measured by the T-square thingy. Really, those things should have a built in laser level.

Our percheron is apparently still growing a bit as well, even though he's five years old. That's fine, so long as it isn't in the feet. With the grandness of his hoofs and his hair on the lower part of his legs, at quick glance he looks like he's wearing gray bellbottoms.

Today is the youngest horse's second birthday, yet we still refer to this nearly half-ton brown mass by her nickname, Baby. From what I've been told, typical horses this age are usually a bit more rambunctious (my mother used to describe me that way, so I understand the phase). However, I have to admit, if her personality (horse, not wife) was any more docile I'd be concerned that she was comatose. She is so mild mannered, but then again so is her appaloosa mother. We have hopes her "terrible twos" will be just fine.

Two years ago, for the entire world to see via a rigged web cam system, our appaloosa gave birth. No it wasn't quite that simple, of course. My wife (who also has quite a docile personality except when I don't pick up after myself), playing the role of equine midwife, had to assist in the birthing by pulling the front hoofs as Baby was emerging. Baby didn't seem at all terribly excited upon arrival, but for me it was one of the most beautiful and disgusting things I'd experienced.

She didn't stand up at first (well, I guess that could apply to baby, mother, and wife) and I couldn't tell how she'd be able to. She looked like a fallen top-heavy Martian lander from War of the Worlds. However, after an hour or so, like some organic Transformer toy, she unfolded, steadied, and rose to a perfect standing position – almost – until flopping back down.

Of course, eventually she did stand, learn to walk, run, eat hay, and poop. And since that night two years ago, when the lilies come up, the forsythia bushes turn bright yellow, and the Bradford Pear trees grow two inches overnight, I'm reminded of when we welcomed a very special addition to our family. It's enough to make me forget taxes for a while.

Twenty
Hail to the Chief

Springtime weather conditions in the midsoutheastern United States can change rapidly. One day may be in the mid-70s and sunny with the local parks full of people enjoying typical outdoor activities, the next may bring a threat of light snow flurries and temperatures in the 30s, producing the usual effect of people running to the grocery store to secure a month's supply of bread and milk. The clash of cold and warm air masses often results in anxious hours filled with hail and tornado warnings.

Waking up to the blasting horn of the weather radio announcing an approaching severe storm is not the most comforting experience. Add in the television weather radar's spinning shear marker indicating a possible tornado nearby and the anxiety greatly increases. During these times, my horse-loving partner and I wrestle with whether to leave the horses in the barn or turn them out. An equine equivalent of a barn doggie door could solve the problem on the surface – and I could design one – but we'd want to ensure either all stayed together in the barn or not.

Recently we endured such a night, with hail two inches in diameter pounding the property. We huddled together with our two dogs in an interior closet while the chunks of ice pounded the roof, sounding like an orchestra of jackhammers. There were multiple storms that night, and in between outbreaks, my equine-loving wife walked to the barn to ensure all ponies were fine. Note to self: must install barn web camera again.

Spring also brings garage sales – lots of them. Sometimes, among the slightly used treadmills, suspect printers, and phones from the nineties that seem to be staples at these events, I find a treasure. One example is the old training wheel I bought for ten cents the year before and repurposed as a gate support. Usefulness, like beauty, lays often in the eyes of the beholder, but when my wife's eyes some of the items I be holding when I return, she usually insists they be removed from the house and deposited in Man's World.

At one recent garage sale, while admiring a collection of rusted pulleys and other odd-shaped implements that reminded me of props from an old Vincent Price movie, I heard an elderly woman's voice address me from behind. "My daddy put that in my barn in nineteen and thirty-eight. Do you know what we used it for?"

My only course of action to avoid embarrassment from having no clue as to the use of the collection was to present my thickest New York accent, thereby successfully (hopefully) conveying my origins as a city dweller Yankee who had never stepped foot on a farm (still not too far from the truth). "I dunno, what's it used for?"

"We used it to put hay in the loft, before bales. You'd clamp the hay here, take this rope, hook it to a mule, and then as the mule walks away from the barn the rope lifts the hay up so it can be unloaded into the loft."

Ah! This was exactly the kind of tool that could significantly reduce the awful back-breaking work of tossing hay bales up to the loft. "Can you use it for bales of hay?" I asked.

She looked at me like I had suddenly sprouted a third eyeball. "Why would you want to that? Hay bales are easy, just toss em' up. Ain't nothin' to it," she said with the confidence of one who likely tossed hay well into her seventies – if still not today.

"Ok . . . ok, I'll think about it," was all I muttered as internally I set about repairing my painfully pierced ego.

"I hope your allergies get better," she said to my initial confusion, before understanding my forced heavy New York accent likely only conveyed the message of stuffed sinuses. I still can easily speak "New York," but only when hanging among other natives from the city for an extended period of time awakens my vocal cord muscle memory.

Often I travel to garage sales for items to use in a manner not originally intended, such as the training wheel. For example, our older mare is currently in heat – a few nights earlier she repeatedly, um, let us know. Well, the barn certainly did have a nice ammonia aroma after that, to be sure, but it got me thinking that I may be able to use an old hose, a tool belt and some additional belts to rig a urine collector and removal tool. I had no luck finding any of those items at the Saturday sales, but I did find a bag of wooden clothespins that, if applied to the nose, could block the unpleasant odor.

As previously mentioned, I need to create a new web camera system. Computers and now wireless transmitters are somewhat common at garage sales. I already have secured just about all of the parts needed for building the new barn web cam system with less than a $20 outlay. The one thing I haven't figured out is how to stop Baby from sticking her tongue out and mooning the camera.

Finding good quality tools is like striking gold at yard sales. A large percentage of my tool inventory comes directly from tooling around early Saturday morning. But on the night of the big hail, it was the simplest of implements that my appaloosa-adoring spouse used to mitigate some of the risks of what could have been a bad situation. In the interim between approaching shear markers and baseball-sized hail, she went out and affixed orange plastic tags with our phone number written in black marker on one hoof of each horse. If the ponies should follow their natural instincts and bolt upon an approaching tornado, when found someone would look at the bright orange tags, see the number, and contact us.

I bet I can build a better tag, with a flashing strobe and GPS enabled . . . but I guess I'll have to wait until I start seeing used GPS navigators at yard sales.

Twenty-One
Horse Show

With nice, warm, sunny spring weather comes the horse show season. To an equine lover, this brings more anticipation than Christmas morning. To an equine lover's spouse, this provides the wonderful opportunity to sharpen one's skills as water bearer, groomer, photographer, and worrier (when watching the spouse guide the horse over rails taller than the bed of our F-250).

I understand there are different types of horse shows, each highlighting a unique set of challenges. Some involve jumping, some artistic expression, some flat out speed. Personally, I never wanted to participate in pony rides at a local amusement park when I was a kid. I could never get over the "staying on without screaming in terror" aspect.

The horse has to look its best, of course. For the last show, my equine-loving wife sculptured her steed's mane to give him what looked to me to be a mohawk. She joked about adding gold chains and changing his show name to "Mister T." I think she may be preparing to enter the percheron in MTV's "Pimp My Ride, Equine Edition." I pity the fool!

Seriously, whatever the competition both horse and rider do need to present a sharp visual presence. The judging of any event involves contemplating the appearance of both equine and human. Emulating Ruth and Festus just would not cut it.

My wife's preferred type of competition is "Three-Day Eventing." After arriving on site and unloading then securing the horse to the side of the trailer to snack on a generous helping of hay in the mesh sack, riders walk the cross-country course. I can understand that it is better for the human half of the team to see the obstacles beforehand to most effectively (and safely) plan the ride, but it does seem a tad unfair that the horse is not afforded the same opportunity. Generally, this traditional stroll occurs quite early in the morning. While usually nothing short of a Big Gulp sized coffee shakes me from my nocturne travels prior to 8 AM, when I accompany my wife on these walks I prefer to remain in the blurry-eyed world of blissful ignorance (see the first paragraph).

Dressage is usually the first of the three events and involves a complex series of walks, trots, and turns in an area roughly the size of a hockey rink. Even though by the time the competition starts I've made it through the majority of my jumbo java, I still usually have trouble understanding the scoring. For me, just being able to start and stop the horse would be worthy of a ribbon.

Between events I am in full support mode, which generally starts with giving my competing partner a bottle of cool water. Proper hydration is certainly quite important, but too much can lead to unscheduled additional business between events. It usually is a necessity for me as an after-effect of extreme caffeine ingestion.

Next is the running of the aforementioned cross-country course. Aiming for accuracy, time, and staying alive, it is thrilling to watch as riders jump over and gallop through streams and other obstacles. Think Evel Knievel jumping the Snake River Canyon. Strike that, bad analogy.

Following another round of providing water and silent prayers, it is off to stadium jumping. So far as I can tell the only difference really between this and cross-country is the ambulance is closer. But steed and rider always come through with flying colors, and the blue usually fades from my face once I resume breathing.

After the events, I like to show my wife the pictures I've taken with our digital camera. Producing decent photographs from a horse show takes skill, patience, and a memory stick that can hold at least 500 pictures, because I'm lucky if 10% of my shots are not blurry, microscopic images of my thumb, or well-centered shots of tails and hoofs. Jimmy Olsen I'm not . . . Superman, where are you now?

After all events have completed and judged comes my favorite part of the competition, the presentation of the awards. At the risk of sounding slightly less than objective, my wonderful equine-loving wife has recently brought home enough blue and red ribbons to give Betsy Ross work for a week. Regardless, I am always bursting with pride at her effort, whether or not a ribbon accompanies us home.

Upon return to the mini-farm, one of the final duties is to unload and feed the horse. My job is to assist by lifting the "butt bar" so that our percheron can gently back himself out of the trailer. While I try to be as attentive as possible, a "backup beeper" would certainly be a great safety addition. For that matter, why can we not load them backwards so they can simply walk forward down the ramp on unloading? I suppose that would mean backing the ponies into the trailer. Or how about installing a "batcave batmobile turner" to reposition the horses while in transit?

While I may not quite understand the draw of "Three-Day Eventing," the most important thing for me is not necessarily to grasp the attraction, rather to simply accept that she who is my horse-jumping wife gets unparalleled thrills out of competing. So long as we maintain an adequate supply of water, health insurance, memory sticks, and coffee, I'm fine with that.

Twenty-Two
Tractor Pull

I had an interesting conversation with a coworker recently following a meeting. It all began with him saying "I'm selling my tractor." Now, the pull of owning a tractor to bush hog our fields, opening the prospect of retiring rider mowers from field duty, is something I cannot ignore, no matter how proud I am of the mower fleet.

I needed to learn more, though, not just about this opportunity, but tractors in general. I'm not so prideful as to not admit that it is she, my equestrian-hopping honey, who is the true expert in these matters. I therefore explained to our potential provider of the almighty PTO that I would have to discuss the situation with her.

I wrote down all of the data he provided about his tractor for sale, feigning understanding. I forwarded her all of the information in an email, but how difficult could this be? I mean, come on, what is a tractor but a mower on steroids? I may not be a smart man, but I know what a mower is (thank you, Forrest Gump).

Her first inquiry hit me like a Nolan Ryan fastball to the head. "Do the tires have calcium carbonate in them?" Ok, all I registered was calcium, and I imagined the tires filled with some dairy product. What if I sliced one of them open by getting too close to a T-post? Oh well, no use crying over spilled milk.

She explained calcium carbonate is used to provide weight to the tires to provide better traction, and that water didn't work because it would expand on freezing and bust through the tires in the winter. I understood. After all, no one likes changing a flat, especially in the cold, and besides I don't think I have a jack big enough to lift a tractor. Would AAA help? I don't think so. They still haven't stopped laughing about my truck-stuck episode, I'm sure.

The next question she asked was whether it had power steering. What kind of a question is that? I don't know, maybe it does, along with other amenities such as heated seats, an MP3 player and a GPS navigator. Honestly, I could probably use the latter. Although we have less than ten acres, I've been known to get lost on our "Ponderosa."

Several with experience in these matters explained to me that power steering can be a necessity particularly in tight spaces, and our fields are not exactly runways. If they were, I could plop my old Cessna down and cut the field with the prop in no time. Yes, I'm still looking for some way to combine flying fun with farm duties.

But I digress, as usual. I'm not sure if the tractor is worth the asking price, about five times what I paid for my first car, a used 1979 AMC Spirit (my car selection skills were not exactly refined as a teenager, but the jalopy had a great stereo). I've been mowing the fields for three years now. That's not exactly what mowers are designed for, but I've hardened the equipment, such as adding reinforcement bars when the mower ran so hot once cutting tall grass and weeds that the exhaust manifold melted the front grill. I can buy a substantial amount of repair materials for the mowers, or even a few new mowers, with the money that this tractor costs.

I'm not even sure how the herd will react to seeing a tractor. Horses seem to be naturally curious animals, and every time I've been mowing a field one usually comes over to try to "help." Maybe they're protective of the field and the grass it contains. If that's the case, they may have let the puny mower go by, but would they rise up against the mighty tractor?

Or perhaps they are studying it, contemplating its use for when they return to human form. Nope, haven't weaned myself from AM late night talk shows yet.

While on the subject, how did farmers manage fields before tractors anyway? I know they used horses and oxen to pull plows, but I never saw Ben Cartwright behind a team pulling an 1800s bush hog. Maybe they did, but the Bonanza folks thought it would make for uninteresting television.

Again I have digressed so far I pulled a muscle in my neck. I'm reluctant, even afraid to plunge into the tractor world. Remember, up until a few years ago I was a city dweller. I could navigate the New York City subway system blindfold, but to think that I'd be pondering a tractor now is like Spock getting ready to race NASCAR. "The yellow flag is not logical, Captain."

The point is though that we really need a tractor. As much as I've enjoyed conditioning old rider mowers for field work, I really do think it's time to graduate to something bigger. We will look at the tractor and maybe take it for a test bush hog. If we opt to make the purchase, it will be a change, that's for sure. Change can be beneficial, especially the spare coins retrieved from between the seats of my truck when I'm in a burger mood and my wallet is running on empty. So, reluctantly, the time has come to give into the tractor pull. At the very least, I'm sure owning and operating one will spawn topics for future articles.

Twenty-Three
Words of the Horse

Becoming the equine expert that I am in my mind did not happen overnight. It required the mastery of terms that were quite unfamiliar to me. Listening to my significant other talk to other horse lovers was often like watching a foreign movie without subtitles. Since I did not possess a Federation Universal Translator, I often had to educate myself the hard way: Google.

Relying on common meanings can produce frightening results. When dating, I distinctly remember my wife-to-be discussing the possibility of a capped hock. I figured she'd reached her limit at the pawn shop paying for tack (I knew what tack was at this time, being the quick study I am). It turns out of course the issue was biological, not economical. That alone raised my interest rate.

I recognized what a flank was from my days in the military and my extensive experience playing Stratego. When I mentioned that a good flanking maneuver is necessary to capture your opponent's flag, I received only a blank stare from my wife in response. I made a mental note to 1) keep my mouth shut and 2) look up "horse + flank" on the Internet.

The resulting search didn't help much, as flank was defined as the portion of the horse behind the barrel. When barrel racing, isn't all of the horse between barrels? Or when jumping barrels, the horse (hopefully) goes over the obstacles. I searched on "barrel" and got "the portion of the horse in front of the flank." So what came first, the barrel or the flank? Of course, I eventually consulted my onsite expert source and she subsequently provided me a lesson in horse physiology.

Once she remarked about how a particular horse's gate was rough. I know much about rough gates, remembering my drawn out, frustrating, but eventually functional repair job on one of our gates. I retrieved from my shed a sledgehammer, spool of twine, and Craftsman 32 piece socket set. She took one look at me and laughed.

Speaking of tools, I suffer a massive amount of tool envy whenever the farrier comes by. That guy has enough tools in his trailer to repair a wrecked Camaro. Jeff Spicoli didn't need his TV repairman father's tools, he needed a farrier's.

Even the word "farrier" had me mixed up. For some time, I thought the word was "ferrier." I figured all of the work the farrier did on the horse's feet were to prepare said horse for a trailer ride to be ferried somewhere.

Then there is the horse show terminology that further confused things for me. When I first started dating my future wife, she was constantly practicing something called "dressage." The only association I could make had to do with clothing, and I knew I was right on the mark when she showed me the pristine suit she was to wear during dressage at her three-day event.

I blocked off three days for this event, which really was held over only two days. She drove across the county to run cross-country and participated in stadium jumping in an arena surrounded by bleachers. Yes, this all made perfect sense.

The word association issues didn't end there and continue to this day. Today my wife asked me to build a coop jump to practice, what else, jumping. I began my project by searching the Internet for Do-It-Yourself plans to build small chicken coops and found one that looked easy enough to construct. I was about to leave for Home Depot to buy some chicken wire when she informed me of my error.

So today, I decided that I needed to do some more research, and proceeded to bookmark several horse dictionary sites. As long as I have a Wi-Fi connection, in an instant I can look like I know what I'm talking about in the equine world. Well, at least I can take a stab at faking it, if my laptop's battery would stop dying.

Twenty-Four
Jump Drive

It's the dog days of summer, and my wife is jumping for joy because she is deep into the eventing season. Me, I'm deep into projects to support her jumping of the equines, which has meant running of the saws, because the more she jumps, the more she wants different obstacles to fly over.

After we had bought the mini-farm, she had mentioned that she needed some jump standards. I remember Carl Lewis had set some high standards in the long jump. I began planning a really long sand pit for the horses before she told me I was thinking horizontally when I needed to be thinking vertically. At least I was thinking.

Jump standards are actually a very simple design. An eight-foot four-by-four cut in half, and a twelve-foot one-by-six cut into eight equal pieces for the base, is all the wood needed to build the standards. Holes bored at equal distances to hold jump cups and a PVC pipe about eight feet long resting in the cups completes the jump. Building these would not require an engineering degree, although I have one just in case.

For whatever reason, my wife wasn't too encouraged by my carpentry skills at the time. Her assessment might be related to my bird feeder creation that resembled a Picasso painting so much squirrels were too afraid to go near it, or perhaps it was the shelf I built that had a natural swinging tendency. Whatever the reason, she required more precision and outsourced the building of the first jumps.

My ego was deflated, my self-esteem was crushed, and my thumb was purple from whacking it with the hammer, but I was determined to learn how to build things that didn't look like I had built them. I sat down and fired up the VCR to study the masters: Bob Villa, Tim Allen, and Bob Ross. OK, I painted some happy trees on my first few projects.

I knew how to operate a handsaw, but needed to fire up power tools. I dusted off the power saw, donned my safety goggles, slung a piece of wood on my sawhorses, and carefully lined up to begin my cut. After a short pause to plug in the saw, I sliced through my first two-by-four. One small step for a man, one large cut for a wanna-be carpenter.

Pretty soon, I was making condemned bird feeders and sloping shelves at a staggering pace. When I discovered the T-square and the level, my accuracy improved dramatically, yet something was still amiss. It was at this time that I learned a two-by-four measured actually about one-and-three-quarters by three-and-a-half. All this time I was getting ripped off by purchasing substandard lumber, I thought. Of course, if I had only researched carpentry a bit, I would have realized these measurements are standard.

With my newly gained skills and knowledge, I produced a bird feeder worthy of my wife's compliment. With pride, I explained the hinged door for adding birdseed and the extended patio for bird socializing. Of course the latter was actually a "happy accident" (thanks again, Bob Ross) but it didn't matter. In my equine-loving spouse's eyes, I was worthy of the next step: building a jump.

One day a few weeks ago, my wife lamented that she always wanted a coop jump. After a minor misunderstanding (see previous chapter), she had printed off plans from the Internet, showed them to me and asked if I felt I could build it. I looked at them and responded with a sly smile that not only can I build it but I could build it fast. Rome wasn't built in a day, but a coop jump would be.

That Saturday morning, I took the oversized manly F-250 diesel to Home Depot and mingled with the other carpenters sizing up their materials lists for their weekend projects. I had joined an elite fraternity, a weekend warrior of the woodworking world. I was with peers, friends even. All would be all right.

The air was right. The table saw, miter saw, and power handsaw were ready, dripping with anticipation of usefulness in building something. There's nothing like the roar of a power saw in the morning; sounds like victory!

I unloaded the wood and studied the printouts. The plans assumed a one-by-six was in fact six inches wide, but I now knew better. I took out my tape measure, protractor, pencil, and paper, and recreated the plans with proper measurements. This was my chance. I was called up to "the show," and I wouldn't blow it. Put me in coach, I'm ready to play!

When I mated the first of four braces together, it was as if the trumpets of angels blared. The pieces of wood fit so perfectly together that not even a starved termite could penetrate that crevice. Having validated the process, I made the other three braces and cut the planks. Time wore on and I could not screw in the planks by hand that night. It was my carpenter supervisor who the next day suggested I use a power screwdriver. What a concept!

I had to complete constructing the jump by mid-afternoon that Sunday, as my wife had invited several other horse-hopping friends to test the coop. With pride, we loaded the finished product into the truck, drove out to the front jump field, and set up the new obstacle within an hour of the arrival of her friends.

I know there will be more and different jumps to build, yet I am not afraid. She has her jump drive, and I have mine. It's plugged into my laptop computer.

Twenty-Five
Wire Services

TESLA COIL, TN (FtL) – My equestrian-captivated wife certainly has more courage than I, at least when it comes to electric fences. She will routinely test our hot wire fence (actually a hot tape) by simply touching it. I avoid that strip of woven wire and plastic like the plague. She knows this, and as part of a diet plan for me she has threatened to hot wire the refrigerator.

"Hot wire" actually had a different meaning for me in high school, but that's another story. I learned of electric fences in college when, while on a road trip that took us through the country, we stopped at an electric pasture fence to look at cows. One of my friends (the one knowledgeable about such fences) said it produced a shock, but I doubted him and grabbed the fence wire. For a fraction of a second, I thought he was wrong, and then the pulse hit. No, I don't care to touch another, thank you.

Of course, I have made contact with our hot tape over the years, just not on purpose. Usually it involved mowing; whether it be maneuvering just a little too close to a fence, opening a gate and unhooking the hot fence connector to drive a mower into a field, or forgetting to unhook said connector and driving the mower into the active hot wire.

Ok, I know I'm really making a big deal out of nothing, but I hate the hot tape. I hate it a lot.

Recently though I discovered the secret behind my wife's seemingly courageous acts of grabbing the wire and holding on – she only does so at a couple of very specific locations. Our fence, with numerous splices, gate hooks, sections literally tied together, and burn through areas, has lost much of its amperage in places, reducing the corresponding shock at some points far away from the charger. It was time to replace much of the hot fence.

Now, there are some things I'm good at, like Sudoku and finding deals at yard sales, but the fence system is my wife's domain. When it comes to equine containment, she is the boss, and thusly designed and assigned me the first repair job. I was to remove a line of twenty-five or so temporary fiberglass poles and associated hot tape, and replace them with ten T-posts, tape holders, and new hot tape.

After shocking myself yet again, then uttering the required follow-up cursing under my breath as I walked to the solar charger to turn it off, I was ready to remove the old hot tape fence. It was temporary, anyway, which meant it had been in place for four years. Have you ever removed four-year-old weathered fiberglass poles? Here's a hint I hope you remember: wear leather work gloves.

After washing the fiberglass splinters off my hands and arms, the red swelling marks began to subside, and I was ready for the T-posts. Pounding T-posts into the ground is a relatively simple task. Funny, I seem to say that all mini-farm tasks are relatively simple, until I learn otherwise. Anyway, the only tool (besides gloves) needed is the "pole banger," essentially a pipe with handles and a sealed end. You place it over the top of the T-post and bang repeatedly. Each bang pushes the T-post a little further into the ground. Or so goes the theory.

Well, after a few taps I figured I could do this much faster if I raised the pole banger above the top of the T-post, thereby increasing the distance and therefore the force. The kinetic energy increases because the velocity increases because of the greater distance. I am an engineer, after all.

When book smarts and street smarts rumble, book smarts usually lose. I did my best Ralph Hinkley in the suit and let the first pound go. And go it did, past the top of the T-post, out of my hands, and smashing into my right shin.

After another round of swearing, I reverted to the "slow and steady" tap method. In short order all T-posts were in the ground, and it was time to install the hot tape holder clips. My favorite-fence-expert explained how to install the clips easily, but I was more concerned about how the Titans were doing. After her soliloquy, I paused the job to go inside for a fresh battery for my headset.

There was an odd synergy between Titans and T-posts that day. Every time I'd try to put on one of those plastic things, it would fly off the pole just as a Titans' receiver would drop a pass. Not wanting to disappoint Jeff Fisher, I recalled my wife's instructions and carefully placed the plastic holder over one edge then slid it around until it clicked on the other edge. Touchdown!

We ran the new tape, turned on the charger, and my wife declared the enhanced pony containment system operational. When I asked her if she was sure, she dared me to touch it if I doubted her. There are times you just need accept the word of your spouse, and this was one of them.

This by no means corrected all of the fence issues, but you cannot have a sequel without a good cliffhanger. I'll discuss advanced electric fence fixing in a future article. For now, I think I'll just watch the next Titans game on TV.

Twenty-Six
A Horse Night Before Christmas

With Christmas fast approaching, stockings hang from every stall in anticipation that Santa Claus will fill them with carrots and other yummy treats. I decided against putting up a small Christmas tree in the barn. If the horses did not eat the branches, the tree would surely become the next paddock toy.

Now, I can say (with some bias, of course) that the ponies have in fact been quite good this year, and deserving of a multitude of Christmas goodies. So, in keeping with the spirit of the season, and with thanks (and apologies) to Clement Clarke Moore, here is what horses may be dreaming of this night before Christmas:

'Twas the night before Christmas, and all through the barn,
Not a creature was stirring, not even a yawn.
The stockings were hung by the stalls with care,
In hope that St. Nicholas would soon be there.

The ponies were nested all snug in their shavings,
Visions of alfalfa igniting their cravings!
Leaving the barn and pushing the wheelbarrow,
I had just finished my chores 'til daylight tomorrow.

When out in the paddock there arose such a clatter,

And I ran from the field to see what was the matter.
Through the gate, I made a mad dash,
Forgetting the hot tape, a spark with a flash!

The moon above cast a pleasant blue glow,
O'er the field I no longer had to mow.
When, what my wandering eyes would see,
Not eight reindeer, but a John Deere ATV.

The four-wheeler driver I knew in a lick,
Excitedly I exclaimed, "It is Saint Nick!"
He gunned the throttle and turned the key,
And the engine backfired, scaring me!

"Now Dasher and Dancer and Prancer and Rudolph,
And all the rest are home goofing off!
Forget milk and crackers, I need fuel,
And in exchange here are gifts of yule."

His offer was certainly quite generous,
If not perhaps a wee bit ridiculous!
"Sure," I replied, not knowing why,
But just then he made that four-wheeler fly!

With a thud the tires landed on the roof,
All dogs responded with a stereophonic "woof."
As I shook my head, turning around,
I knew how crazy this story would sound.

He wore leather from his head to his foot,
A throwback to the 60s was his enormous boot!

A round bale he had flung on his back,
And just for that feat I would give him no flack.

His eyes, how they twinkled, and his dimples, how merry!
Yet he had to unload his gifts in a hurry.
Slowly he steadied himself on the roof,
Then slipped and fell, landing with an 'Oof!"

A riding crop he held tightly in his teeth,
"I used to ride but lately I've been weak."
I offered the appy for a short trail ride.
"She's gentle and kind and will stick by your side."

He was chubby and plump, a right jolly old elf,
And I laughed when I watched him try to ride by himself!
"I have to admit," he said with some dread,
"I always use the autopilot in my sled!"

He spoke no more words, and cantered with a jerk,
But the horse was nice and did all the work.
Soon he dismounted and left hay and gifts,
Then gunned the ATV and drove off very swift!

I surveyed the barn and marveled at it all,
The overflowing stockings in front of each stall.
A sound bellowed from the ATV's fading taillight,
"Merry Christmas to all, and to all a good night!"

Twenty-Seven
Back in the Saddle

More time than usual has passed since I wrote a column, and I know that there may be questions as to the reasons for my absence. So, my first business is to quickly dispel any possible rumors. No, the loft did not fall down, nor did I audition for American Idol, nor did I return to my city roots. Actually, the reason is quite simple: we finally bought a tractor.

I know I've talked (and written) about doing so for years, and actually came close to purchasing one from a friend last summer. The bottom line though is that I was afraid of the bottom line. The power of a tractor as compared to a riding mower, I'll admit, also intimidated me somewhat. Wait, scratch that. I won't admit that, even if it's true, lest I lose my Man Club membership card.

No, actually the reason was pure evolution, or perhaps internal revolution (or internal combustion). We had an early spring, which meant an early mow. In my youth, a normal February up north meant keeping the snow shovel close by, but this year in the south grass cutting would commence weeks before tax day.

And so I began the spring ritual of prepping the mowers for yard and field work. Naturally, the primary mower (the green one) had a dead battery. Confident it would start after a good charge, I hooked up a trickle charger to the battery. The next morning, eager to cut new grass with jumbo java in hand, I turned the key, heard a click, then nothing. I put the battery back on the charger, drank my coffee, and tackled Sudoku, confident that tomorrow would bring success.

The next morning, once again with coffee in hand, I unhooked the charger, reconnected the battery, and turned the key – click, then nothing. I did this a few more times, with the same result. Albert Einstein allegedly once defined insanity as the process of doing the exact same thing and expecting different results, so I guess I was in need of some help. Naturally, I consulted the mower manual.

I determined the solenoid was toast. The grass really needed cutting, so I deferred a trip to Home Depot and turned to the five dollar yard sale special, which had been sitting in the pole barn for months without so much as a thought. Yet, on the first try, it cranked up fine and I was able to mow the yard with a 20-year-old refurbished yard sale mower while the five-year-old store bought new one sat useless.

Well, that would have been fine except when I decided to push the green mower back to the shed to await the new solenoid, the rear tires decided not to move. During the week or so it spent sitting while I charged the battery multiple times, the transmission seized. This insubordination threw me over the edge as I uttered some words that I never knew existed.

That night I told my country wife that I was fed up with the mowers and with the prospect of mowing the fields another year, and wanted to buy a tractor. Obviously, Einstein was correct, as my wife thought I'd flipped my lid. But she was determined to strike while the iron was hot. A tractor proponent since we moved to the mini-farm, she patiently let me spend years mowing the fields and yard while she plotted her strategy. It wasn't more than an hour after I blurted out my desire to buy a tractor that she was at a tractor dealership.

You see, she who would become my tractor-trainer knew already exactly what she wanted. Some husbands' mates dream of a fur coat or fine jewelry, but my horse-loving honey yearned for a tractor. She gathered all of the information on the model and attachments she felt we needed and prepared to meet me after work, lest my moment of insanity wears off.

Well, when I got home that day and saw the green mower sitting there, partially disassembled, I imagined it mocking me. I kicked the front end hard in frustration, and then hobbled up the stars into the house.

My wife had placed the tractor marketing material as well as the cost estimate on the dining room table, knowing I would pass by there. She explained to me the necessity of a finishing mower and a bush hog, why hydrostatics is better, and the benefit of having a front-end loader, but all I cared about by this point was the cup holder.

The beverage stabilizer was indeed sweet: dual size, with conforming plastic to minimize shaking. A master of engineering it was, and so I told her I would probably stop by the dealership the next day to sign, but I wanted to sit in it first and try out the cup holder. By this point in time I am sure my wife was seriously considering making me see a therapist, but after buying the tractor, of course.

The dealership delivered the tractor a few days later. With a bit of uncertainty, I started it. Let me state the obvious: this was one huge riding mower!

But would it really help with the chores? One of the fields needed cutting. With a forlorn expression I'm sure, I glanced at the red mower, mounted the tractor, and engaged the PTO. The bush hog roared to life, and I began cutting. I was done in a fraction of the time than the mower would have taken.

I was like the tractor – sold. Henceforth, every opportunity I could leverage to use the tractor, I did, perhaps at the expense of other activities, including writing. It's uses seem limitless. For example, it was pretty cool when I used the front end loader and a couple of heavy-duty chains to remove bushes. My wife just rolled her eyes when I told her I was considering getting a backhoe attachment.

Twenty-Eight
It's All Relative

Recently my immediate family visited us at the mini-farm to surprise me for my birthday – one of those major ones that end in zero. This marked the first time my two brothers and their families had visited any equine household, and likely the first time they had encountered horses outside of a race track or a carriage ride. The closest my brothers and I ever got to a horse as children was riding a carousel at a local amusement park.

I am the equine-expert compared to my relatives, of course. I was definitely not going to let this opportunity to show off my extensive equine knowledge pass by. So, with my brothers in tow, we entered a field to lead the ponies to the barn for their dinner.

Well, truth is, both of my siblings remained at the gate at what they perceived as a safe distance, while I led the two horses into the barn. They were more comfortable saying hello to the ponies separated by a heavy, latched stall door, and I was fine with that. I appreciated their wise judgement, as they were not accustomed to the close proximity of the large animals. One even compared our percheron's girth to a subway car's width. I don't think any feelings were hurt.

Eventually I convinced both to mingle with the ponies with me after turning them out following dinner. Of course, I had snuck a few yummy treats into one brother's jacket pocket. He took a few moments to figure out why he was the sole recipient of some extra equine affection.

One asked if the purpose of the white ribbons tied to the electric fence was to act as a visual cue to avoid the wire. I confirmed his suspicions and had started to explain why when he grabbed the wire with one hand. He will not ever forget that shocking experience.

The other found contentment in bouncing in the seat of our tractor as it sat stationary near the barn entrance. He apparently learned such was the correct method to riding a tractor from the opening credits of Green Acres. I explained posting was not necessary when operating the machine, then had to explain what posting was. But he remained enthralled by the tractor. And why not? It was a Tonka Toy on steroids; how could that not bring out the little boy in a grown man?

But I really enjoyed introducing my two young nieces to horseback riding. I will never forget their looks of sheer delight, as if Christmas had come in June. Sometimes the simpler things in life really are the best and most memorable. Explaining that they could not take a horse home because one would not fit in the airplane's overhead bin took a bit of effort, however.

The girls were really into learning about the horses. My wife explained the process of cleaning the muck out of the hoofs and shoes when the younger one asked "Why not take them off and place them in the washing machine?" I guess kids really do say the darndest things. Right Art?

Twenty-Nine
Baby Goes to College

Where does the time go? It seems like just yesterday that I was witnessing my first equine birth live, or at least those parts when I wasn't turned away, pretending to be fiddling with the web camera. That day we welcomed our new baby into the world was three-and-a-half years ago, yet she still carries the nickname of Baby today.

Since that day, Baby has learned to walk, grew to be much larger than her mother, experienced the lunge rope for the first time, and figured out how to eat a carrot. But while home schooling is great, we knew Baby would eventually require the professional education we couldn't provide ourselves to prepare her to become a master eventer. It was time to send Baby to "college," a training farm where she will learn the finer points of being under saddle.

We hadn't saved for college, but it was the idea that Baby would leave our home, if only for three months, that made me uneasy. She had never traveled beyond the mini-farm in her short life. Since day one, she and I have had a special bond. I guess you could say she is "Daddy's Girl." I would make sure she wouldn't date anyone until she was at least five.

Yet here she was, preparing to go away to school way too early. I remembered my experiences and tried to collect the wisdom of my college years to pass on to her. First and foremost on the advice list was no wild parties; I don't care how good the hay looks, you have to know your limit. I also made it quite clear that if she didn't get good grades, we were not going to pay her tuition.

I wasn't home when she left. I told my wife that I had to work later that evening, but truth is I just wasn't strong enough to deal with Baby's inevitable whining when she realized she was leaving. It turns out, according to my wife, that Baby just popped on the trailer, happy to go away to school. Maybe the promise of high speed Internet in her dorm stall enticed her.

Fast-forward two weeks, and it's time for my first visit to the school. We parked at the visitor's center of the sprawling campus and walked through the dorm barn to the paddocks to find Baby hanging out with a couple other young horses.

Now, my equine-enamored wife told me prior to leaving our house that Baby would be glad to see me. However, when we saw her, she ignored me as if to say to her new friends, "It's my father. I wish he hadn't worn those 'old man shorts' again. I'm so embarrassed!"

She eventually acknowledged us and left her friends to greet us at the gate. Once she was inside the dorm barn and out of sight from her friends, she reverted to "Daddy's Girl" behavior.

I'm proud of the grades she has achieved thus far – an A in Basic Saddle, an A minus in Lunge 1, and an A in Trailers and Other New Environments. I'm not too concerned about her C+ in her elective,

Selective Grass Encounters, as she's taking that one Pass/Fail.

It was late and she had an evening class so we took some quick pictures and led her back to the dorm barn. Almost as soon as we had arrived, we were preparing to leave. She seemed to be glad to see me, but after we walked her back to the paddock, she took off to be with her friends.

It's tough to let them leave the nest, but I know that she'll do well in this world with a college education. Maybe next time when I visit I'll wear some more fashionable shorts and ditch the black socks. In any case, I'll definitely bring some carrots . . . so long as she keeps her grades up.

Thirty
Racing Stripes

I love this time of year, as summer migrates to autumn. There is a slight crispness in the air, the fields no longer require bush hogging, and all winter hay is tossed and stacked in the loft. This fall is a bit different than past years at the mini-farm, though. With Baby still away at school and having found a home for our rescue horse project, we're down to two horses. Life is quieter, but even I can handle chores for two horses with relative ease.

Recently because of a business trip that took her out of town, my wife handed the reigns of horse care to me for a few days. As is customary, she reviewed with me the chores and duties necessary to keep the ponies happy and healthy. Actually, I've been caring for the animals for so many years that I really have developed a good feel for it, but she has the equine-expert eye and adjusts feed and other details based on a variety of factors.

For example, things get a bit complicated this time of year because it can be cold at night and warm during the day. The temperature variation means my horse-loving honey whips out her multi-layered blanketing strategy. Between one range of degrees the thin blanket is applied, another range has a thicker blanket, and if it gets below zero the horses usually just log on to Priceline.com and book a trip to the Bahamas.

Blanketing only comes into play if the horses are clipped. Clipping the winter coat helps to ensure that the horse won't overheat when ridden, but it also removes a natural barrier to the cold. One of the two is not ridden much anymore, so we generally let her keep her full coat, but the other my wife rides regularly and therefore underwent "shear pleasure."

Now, she is so skilled with the clippers that she could have been a master barber. She can give a pony a high and tight that any Marine would be proud of. She actually has cut my hair before but I'm not in the crew cut phase currently. Thus, her clipping skills are for the ponies only, although I still have a mild fear of waking up with a "reverse Mohawk" one morning if I really get on her bad side. Since I love my hair the way it is, I make sure we never go to sleep mad.

So we're going through our ritual of her making sure I know where the hay is (I do; I put it there), the need to scoop poop (I can accurately toss it into a muck bucket at 15 feet), and so on, when I noticed that one of the horses looked two-toned. No, a better description is that he looked like a superhero in uniform. Half of his body (the lower half) was clipped, the other half wasn't.

"Are you planning to finish his clip job before you leave?" I innocently asked.

"Uh, it's done. It's a trace clip. It allows for ventilation so he doesn't get so hot when he gets worked."

Now, if I get hot when "I'm worked," I reach for a cool drink or jump in the pool. But since it is considered poor behavior for a horse being worked to suddenly dive into a lake, particularly if under saddle, heat dissipation is important. Still, the trace clip gave the horse a streamlined look. The cut sort of looked like racing stripes.

If a horse could have racing stripes, why not follow the NASCAR model and sell advertising space on the horse? Perhaps we can add something like "Tony's Oats" on the side and "Hay Heaven" across the nose. The endorsements alone could pay for a new barn.

As I was finishing writing this article, my partner informed me she also has created a new feeding schedule for our dogs. She is very detail oriented when it comes to animal care, which is a good thing, I'll admit. But I wonder – will our dogs getting racing stripes, too? After all, our little Jack Russell already has a jacket – but does little work.

Thirty-One
Horse Sickness

I am home from work for several days due to an early winter bout with the flu. When you experience complete down time, with an appetite for activity no more strenuous than watching TV, your mind can wander to strange places. Adding in a fever leads to some very interesting, if possibly disturbing thoughts along the sickness imagination highway . . .

Horses never have to drive to work. Most enjoy careers that begin and end in their home pasture. Oh sure, occasionally one may leave for some type of competition or the enjoyment of a trail ride, but generally the horse commute is very short – a few feet from stall to field.

But if horses did have to commute some distance to work, what would they drive? They would certainly require a vehicle with plenty of foot, uh, hoof room. A large SUV may fit the bill. A true horse horseless carriage . . .

Horses do not have much of a morning routine. I would love to one day simply roll out of bed and start work, without such obstacles as shaving, showering, or obsessing over what to wear. Actually, probably some believe I do that anyway.

Take shaving for example. An average shave takes about five minutes, when you factor in waiting for the water to heat up, wiping off the stray shaving cream remaining on the face and neck, and addressing razor nicks. Over the course of twelve months, that's thirty hours a year spent removing hair from the face. No wonder horses seem so happy! I could let the beard grow and the time saved would allow for the viewing of ten more football games.

Of course, lying in bed watching TVLand for several days in a row and occasionally pondering equines in human situations is not exactly the most productive use of down time, but 1) at least my mind was active and 2) that is why it's called "down time." But I do wonder what a horse does to pass the time while sick. Do horses even get the flu? Should they get flu shots? One thing was certain, I needed to get better soon, or else I would slowly drive myself insane.

I am going on record as stating the blatant unfairness that human doctors do not make house calls anymore, but veterinarians do. As the flu dug in for an extended stay, to satisfy my employer I had to visit my doctor so he could verify what I already knew – I was sick. Yet if we suspect a horse is ill, the vet is on site merely minutes after a call – well, maybe hours, but you get the point. Maybe next time I'll call a vet when I get sick.

I am sure there are downsides to being a horse, but thus far I have found none – no commute, no shaving, doctor house calls when ill . . . sounds pretty darn good to me. You also do not need to bother with grocery shopping, as from the horse's' perspective the human(s) always provide the food. Humans of course have to purchase fifty pound feed bags from stores, toss down hay from a supply in a loft (after having lifted the hay up there to begin with), and struggle to push huge round bales off of trucks. The more I ponder, the surer I am that I exist below the horse on the evolutionary chain.

I am a little green with horse envy. Well, no, I'm a little green because I have the flu. Certainly, horses seem to have it made in the shade, but there are some downsides to the equine existence. For example, they do not have cable TV. Even if I did install TV in their stall, good luck trying to operate the remote without an opposable thumb.

Barns (well, ours at least) lack heating and air conditioning systems. I would have loved air conditioning growing up in the brutal high humidity New York summer days, and today cannot imagine life without it. As for heat, one would think enduring ten years of Buffalo winters would have resulted in permanent immunity to sub-freezing temperatures, but the opposite is true. I cannot stand the cold. No, I would not do well as a horse.

As I groggily watch another episode of "I Love Lucy," firmly under the influence of Nyquil, I cannot shake the strong sense of déjà vu. Have I written on this topic before? Have I seen Lucy throw out Ricky's comfortable clothes before? Has my wife thrown out my comfortable clothes? Have I shattered my personal fever record of 103.6? Have I rambled too long?

That's enough for now. The flu has me firmly in its grip, and it is time for another shot of medicine. I look forward to more visions of hay bales dancing in my head.

Thirty-Two
The Sword of Fescue

I don't generally get too excited about anything hay related. I see hay as only horse fuel, grass carcasses that need to be moved and positioned many times after cutting until they finally meet the mouth of a horse. Moving the hay can sometimes be quite difficult, hence my mild disdain for anything hay related.

When we began dating, I tried to impress my future wife with my physical prowess by throwing several bales of hay up to the loft where she boarded her horses. Actually, I think I got more brownie points just for showing my interest in her equine lifestyle, and didn't need to astonish her with feats of barnyard brawn. Of course, after lofting all of the bales up to the loft and dropping her off at her apartment, I stopped by Walgreens to pick up extra-strength ibuprofen for my painful shoulder.

Fast-forward ten years, and I'm still moving hay around in support of my horse-loving wife's passion. Pride does not prohibit me from admitting that I'm a bit slower and tire a bit easier than a decade earlier. Well, maybe I don't, but I get more sympathy if it looks like I'm about to need medical attention. I do seem to finish a bottle of ibuprofen faster.

But moving round bales of high quality horse hay is another story. For the most part, human power alone cannot alter the location of those grass behemoths. Sure, you can roll them if the ground is flat and dry enough, but even that is tough. It provides entertainment for the ponies though, watching their human grunt and puff repositioning days of nourishment.

Now, regular readers of "From the Loft" know that I was quite excited when my wife agreed to, uh, no, when she insisted that we buy a tractor last spring. Since then, I have become perhaps not an expert at tractor operations but at least competent. I haven't ripped apart any fencing yet with the front-end loader, and am quite good at swapping out implements (mainly finishing mower, tiller, and bush hog).

My wife has been lobbying to procure another tractor tool, a hay spear, claiming such would make hay movement easier. At first, I thought this addition to the tractor arsenal was not necessary. Unlike the other implements we own, a hay spear has no moving parts. I started to walk down the road to convince myself that I could build one, but my wife threw the red challenge flag on that idea. On further review the idea of having 800 pounds of grass carcasses fly out of control because of a design or a construction flaw killed that plan.

Thus, when she arrived home with the hay spear, I was actually looking forward to trying it. I hooked it on the tractor easily enough, as it's really a simple piece of machinery, one large spear and two smaller ones on the bottom to aid in round bale stability. I wanted to make sure I had mounted it correctly and did a test-drive around the yard. There was only one minor incident, when I backed it into a maple tree, but that worked out for the best – we tapped the resulting hole for syrup later on.

    The time came to move a round bale from a covered area to the field – this new "Sword of Fescue's" first true test. There is a basic law of farm duties, it seems: the easier something looks, the harder it is. You'd think that backing a hay spear into a round bale and lifting it up would be simple. However, the first attempt only pushed the bale back about five yards without getting a firm hold on it.

    Our horses were standing by the fence watching me, undoubtedly enjoying all of this. I'm sure they were laughing inwardly as I considered that perhaps the main spear needed to penetrate the center of the bale. This only made sense and may have been part of the instructions but for some reason I didn't read the booklet that came with the implement.

    This time the spear slid in only about halfway before the bale started to tip. Raising and lowering the three-point hitch didn't have much effect, so I set it down and tried again. Long story short, after much trial and error I successfully inserted the spear in the center and was able to transport the bale out to the pasture. The ponies were glad and they followed me like I was a fescue pied piper as I drove the tractor into the field and deposited the bale on the ground.

    Dinner wasn't ready yet, however. I still had to tip the bale so it rested on a flat end, cut the hay strings, and surround it with the ring. All are basic tasks, but tipping the round bale can sometimes be tricky, particularly if the ground is muddy, as was the case that day. Before I got off the tractor though, I had a thought. It should be easy to use the front-end loader to tip the bale. Now, reread my thoughts on seemingly easy farm tasks above. However, this proved to be the exception to the rule, and the bale tipped nicely with just a gentle nudge.

As I drove the tractor back to the barn, I sensed that the ponies were pleased with my work and their dinner. For us, a healthy horse is a happy horse. And if getting to that point also preserves my shoulder health, I'm all for it.

Thirty-Three
Baby Comes Home

My, how time flies. The little ones grow up so fast. It seems like just yesterday that our youngest horse, Baby, was wobbling her way up on her legs for the first time. Now she is a college graduate.

When she was born nearly four years ago, I think one of the things that amazed me the most was how such a large animal could have come from her mother. The mechanical engineer in me recognized the excellent packing design of a pre-birth horse in a womb. It reminded me of my college days when I'd return home with all of my life belongings and several loads of dirty laundry loaded in my AMC Spirit. I never needed airbags; if I got into an accident, the laundry would deploy to form a tight protection zone.

But back to Baby. She recently returned home after finishing her schooling. Gone for several months, she majored in "Under Saddle" and minored in "Lead Changes." Thankfully, while I was worried she'd spend too many late nights out with her friends gorging hay, she proved she was mature and took her schooling seriously. I guess she doesn't take after me.

It has been lonely without Baby around. She bonded fast to my equine-loving wife and me since day one when she first unfurled her gangly legs like solar panels on the International Space Station. Of course, we were the first people she saw, but if webcams worked two ways, she would have bonded with several dozen others watching the birth live over the Internet.

She grew fast but never seemed to have an awkward personality (horseonality?) season. My horse-loving mate and I expected Baby to go through phases acting like, well, a young horse, yet she never had "Ornery Ones," "Terrible Twos," or "Trashy Threes." Again, not taking after me . . .

She definitely enjoyed growing up on the mini-farm with her biological mother and adopted brother. They played, ate hay, and ran together. The work require to mow, and later bush hog (I can never say enough how glad I am that we got a tractor) the fields to give her and her two family members a nice, healthy living area is worth it. I know they appreciate their clean fields. That logic also works with a significant other when picking up items strewn around the house.

Now, though, she needs to understand that she has a job to do, that life isn't free of responsibilities. Her future involves many horse shows and trail rides, meaning she must sharpen her new skills and stay fit. Lounging around watching "Hee Haw" DVDs won't cut it.

Her transition from college to the real world of on-the-job training has been rather smooth, but there have been a few bumps. One time last week Baby decided that, despite having never had an issue trailer loading previously, she did not want to cooperate. Once we pulled out her job description and showed it to her, she realized that sometimes we must perform tasks in our career that we don't necessarily enjoy.

I know she is concerned about keeping her job, given the state of the economy. She recognizes that such attractive positions are difficult to come by, what with all of the benefits included (room and board, health care, Internet service, and so on). But that doesn't mean she's not worried. She diversified her retirement plan once again yesterday, having realized she was top heavy in carrot futures.

The most important thing though is we, her adoptive parents, and her birth mother raised her well enough that we're sure she can handle herself out there. She will always be "Daddy's Girl," of course. There will be serious vetting of the stud who asks me for her hoof in paddock, uh wedlock.

Thirty-Four
Enter the Donkey!

My wife has often stated that, ever since childhood, she has wanted a donkey. When asked why, she would always reply that she had no concrete reason, just a desire. I accepted her answer on the same level of my mid-life crisis wish to own a Corvette – nice to imagine, not likely to happen.

Over the years, the donkey talk would come up, but it was always just talk. Still, I guess in the back of my mind I knew it was only a matter of time before her dream of having a donkey would happen. Thus, when she said a friend had a cute five-month old male donkey that she would let us have for free, I wasn't surprised when she lobbied for us to take him in. A couple of days later, she informed me that the donkey was being delivered. By what, Pony Express?

When I returned home that evening, I was greeted by the sound of a car trying to start followed by a sick old man. When one lives in the country, all noises are noticeable, unobstructed by the hum of human activity. But this one was unnatural . . . almost alien.

I soon learned that donkeys are not born with the ability to bray; they develop it as they grow. I would have to get used to that alien, car-starting, man-dying sound, as would the neighbors. We should have warned them about the donkey, as the first night we had him, his "bray wannabe" apparently startled them enough to consider calling the county sheriff.

I wasn't sure what to expect when I first went to feed the donkey in the paddock (we opted to, at least at first, keep the new arrival separated from the horses for safety). Really, my only experiences with donkeys included watching Quick Draw McGraw cartoons (his sidekick was a donkey, right?) and visiting petting zoos. But here was this fuzzy big dog with jack rabbit ears. Would he be friendly, stubborn (mules get it from somewhere), or wild?

With trepidation, I approached the source of the alien sound. I gently raised my hand to pet him but he flinched and moved backwards, so I crouched down to make myself look less intimidating. As a "vertically challenged" person, I'm not used to my height, or lack thereof, intimidating anything.

That seemed to work, and instantly we became friends. I didn't realize until our interaction that donkeys are actually very personable, or at least this one is. Now that I had gained his trust, he started following me around everywhere in the paddock. The dog analogy was closer than I thought.

Our horses were not as sure about the new addition, therefore we planned gradual introductions and interactions. I know some about horse social behavior and confirmed with my wife the donkey, as an equine, would likely be accepted as part of the herd. Sure enough, Baby quickly bonded with the donkey . . . maybe she felt that she now could assert the "big sister" role, no longer being the youngest. In short order the other two also accepted the donkey into the herd. If only breaking into cliques in high school had been so easy.

The donkey does have his quirks. For a few weeks, he hated crossing the runoff creek when the horses opted to move to the other side for optimum grazing opportunities. He'd stand on the side, run around and buck as well as a six-month-old donkey could. Then would come the car starting / man-dying sound, and he'd jump (sort of) across the creek.

Baby, for whatever reason, has grown to love to use our footbridge over the creek. I built the thing to hold one horse but we have seen two on it at times, a credit to my excellent design, engineering, and construction skills (and my inflated ego). I should have predicted the donkey would also start using the footbridge. Guess I need to start describing it as a hoof bridge.

I'm not sure how she does it, but my wife seems to have an uncanny knack of introducing things to me that I'm afraid I won't like but eventually come to love. In the past, I never really cared for small dogs, but I wouldn't trade our Jack Russell Terrier for anything. So it is with the donkey. He's a treat to have on the farm, and I enjoy going out to just hang out with him. Now, if my wife would only bring home a Corvette.

Thirty-Five
Hay Day

As we grow older, things that used to frighten us, such as the never-seen monster under the bed or the first day of school, lose their hold on our fear. I have hardened with the progression of time, but I still dread the first day of summer, known here on the mini-farm as Hay Day.

Lest you think, dear reader, that I am overly paranoid, let me assure you my trepidation is well founded. As I write this, both my hay-haulin' honey and I are lounging on the couch after a very satisfying pizza dinner. The occasion is not a COPS marathon but rather recovery from a day of acquiring, stacking, transporting, throwing, and again stacking square hay bales.

Last year, a late spring freeze coupled with a very hot, dry summer caused hay demand, and therefore prices, to skyrocket in many areas of the southeast United States. But this spring is one of the greenest I have ever seen. The trees are lush, water levels in reservoirs are up to normal, and Memorial Day weekend was punctuated with hay cutting and baling everywhere I looked while driving through the countryside.

My wife may have been a squirrel in a previous life judging by the way she pays attention to storing horse food for the coming winter staring in the early summer. Equines need hay when grass does not grow in the fall and winter, necessitating a full supply of hay before the leaves come off the trees. The Great Hay Shortage last year displayed the need for "squirrelling away" as much hay as possible. There would be no hot dogs and beer this Memorial Day.

Today, ibuprofen is my best friend once again. My forearms look as if they have been shot with several dozen BBs (if you have tossed hay without wearing long sleeves you understand). The simple action of rising and walking to the kitchen requires extra effort as every joint in my body seemingly cries for some ibuprofen.

While I love our equines (I cannot say "horses" anymore as the limiting term would offend our seven-month old donkey), sometimes I wish they could eat dirt instead of hay. We have an ample supply of mineral-enriched soil. But alas, horses (and donkeys) require hay.

In fact, the only upside to Hay Day is in providing a theme for this month's column. While throwing bales up to my wife receiving them at the loft door, I realized that while my nose was stuffy from the hay, my writer's block had cleared.

Thus, I get to whine and you get to read about my complaining, and hopefully I'm the only one in pain. In our early courtship days, I tried to impress my future wife with my ability to throw hay bales like they were kickballs. These days I impress myself if I wake up in the morning, and she's impressed if I do the dishes. The macho idea of flinging hay like I was a twenty-something is as dated as a Dukes of Hazzard car chase.

Today's plan was to load square bales from a field on to a borrowed flatbed trailer, carefully tie the bales down, drive the thirteen-point-six miles to our mini-farm, and unload the trailer by using it as a platform to chuck the bales up to the barn's loft. My shoulder protested in pain from loading roughly a hundred bales of hay on the flatbed. But I needed a better solution for stocking the loft and defeat my other arch-nemesis, gravity. With no hay elevator available to move bales from trailer to loft, inspiration struck. Enter the tractor!

More specifically, enter the tractor's front-end loader. I will be the first to admit that I loudly protested adding the implement when we bought the tractor – I just did not see the value in the extra expense. Listen (read) carefully – I was wrong. Three bales fit perfectly into the bucket, and while it took some time, we finished the restocking job with the help of the loader.

We certainly earned the pizza and the couch lounging time. Now I think I'll take a nap, and try to dream up more ways that I can stock our equines' winter pantry. And as I stared to doze off, I saw out the window a squirrel running on the rail of our front porch, acorn in its mouth.

Thirty-Six
Something in the Water

Those nights when I come home late from work my equine-loving wife is often still at the barn, having finished riding or performing some horse related chore. Our impromptu barn conversations usually consist of small talk. Tonight though I had more work to accomplish (namely, writing this article) and said that I just came over to say hello.

"Well, I didn't think you were coming to clean stalls," she replied.

Now, I could have taken that several ways, but it was obvious she meant the comeback in a joking manner. At least I hoped so, because I didn't pick up a hay rake. So, while she was gathering manure into the wheelbarrow, I opted to employ "the best defense is a strong offense" strategy. "Is the wheelbarrow working fine for you now?"

You see, I had fixed the wheelbarrow this past weekend by fashioning some spacers out of PVC tubing to keep the wheel from sliding on the axle. While I was of course interested in if she was pleased with the fix, that wasn't my main reason for asking. I knew it worked fine because, well, I fixed it. No, I had to remind her that I had in fact added to my barn chore karma this week, thereby ensuring the fixed wheelbarrow would act as a deflector shield, rendering any "stall cleaning suggestion torpedo" ineffective.

Having avoided any chance of her coercing me into barn work, we returned to small talk. She suggested that there must be something in the water. I asked her what she meant, hoping she was not leading up to suggesting I clean the trough.

"Our percheron just cannot stop playing in the trough."

Before you crystallize that mental image, no, she didn't mean that the percheron jumps in like the trough is a swimming pool. He's not that small and the trough isn't that big. Remember, he likes to "hoof" at the water with his two front legs. He'll stand there and happily splash for minutes at a time.

Because that dirties the trough, however, a request for cleaning remained a possibility. I had to quickly think fast and add redundantly repetitive words to lengthen the small talk. I asked her to expand on her thoughts.

"Well, the little pup does the same thing with his water dish when he's out, and you know our lab would stay in the pool all day if we had one," she explained. "Heck, look at the foxes; they were out in the creek playing last week."

She's right, of course. I looked across the fence to our back yard, and the Jack Russell Terrier was flopping in the little tub we set out for him. Even one of our cats was drinking, and drinking, and drinking. It does seem like something in the water here may be affecting the animals, making them more playful and active.

Hmmm.

Wait a minute. Last time we got hay, my wife encouraged me to take several water breaks. Now that I think about it, when I was bush hogging the back field and was about to quit, she suggested I have a nice cold glass of iced tea that was made with, yup, our water. And when we celebrated our anniversary at home last month, we didn't toast with wine, but with water.

Maybe something in our water produces more energy, like a modern day Fountain of Youth. "Honey, is there something about our water that I don't know about?" I asked. She simply shrugged her shoulders and smiled as she offered me a cup of water and a hayfork.

My pulse was racing and my heart was pounding in my chest. I ran from the barn in a panic, past the horses as it suddenly started raining, then pouring. Everywhere I went I was getting wet, even inside the house! Suddenly I found myself in bed, drenched in sweat, panting. My wife groggily leaned over and asked what was wrong.

"I had a dream that there was something in the water that made me do horse chores."

"You need to stop watching 'X-Files' reruns before bed."

I realized that there is no water conspiracy theory here. The horses, dogs, and foxes are just doing what comes naturally, being playful. I was genuinely thirsty after working. No, all was normal, and it was just a bad dream. As I lay back down, she reached over and held something in front of me.

"Here, have a nice cold glass of water."

Somewhere outside in the darkness, a horse whinnied.

Thirty-Seven
Runaway

There always appears to be an endless list of chores and projects at the mini-farm, but sometimes I just need an afternoon of nothing. A Star Trek marathon on TV provided the perfect excuse to take a few hours to recharge.

While reclining in my favorite chair, watching Captain Picard riding dressage, I pondered what differences the 24th century would bring to the sport. My equine-loving wife is not much of a fan of Star Trek, but I'd bet she would give the show more than a quick glance if she knew they predicted three-day eventing would still exist 300 years in the future.

Dozing in and out, at one point I thought I heard horses whinny a few times, but figured it was related to Picard's poor riding. Then I heard what sounded like someone calling for help. I looked out the window to see a figure dressed in britches and a riding helmet lying face down on the ground. Immediately I had a flashback to that moment several years ago when I had learned my wife had fallen off a horse and broke her ankle in several places.

At some point my wife must have come home while I was asleep and opted to ride and fell again, I thought as I raced outside in my pajama pants and T-shirt. When I arrived at the fallen woman, I realized it was not my wife, rather a friend of ours who occasionally keeps her horse here in exchange for cleaning stalls and performing other small barn chores. It works out well for her as she can use our field and jumps to practice, and I get out of some of the horse care duties.

But I digress from the main story. She slowly sat up unassisted, more concerned about her horse's well-being than her own. Noticing that her horse was standing in our driveway (we have a very long driveway so he wasn't near the street, yet), I ordered our friend not to move and set out to retrieve the pony.

Now, this is real life, not the way these types of scenes play out in the movies. Instead of dressed in leather with a three-day's beard growth, dusty boots, and a shirt that hadn't seen a wash in too long, I found myself running after a rather large horse wearing a 3 o'clock shadow, somewhat clean crocks, and a T-shirt that hadn't seen a wash in too long. If it wasn't for the seriousness of the situation, I would have thought that Alan Funt (or his grandson, I guess) was about to appear.

To digress for a moment again, a few days earlier my tractor-tooling honey was mowing our back yard with the finishing mower attached to the PTO (see, I'm learning this farm lingo stuff) when she (well, the roll bar) hit and knocked down a sizeable branch from a large hackberry tree. When I asked her what had happened she repeatedly exclaimed that she didn't hit it hard, and pointed to what looked like rot in one end of the branch. After both chastising and making fun of her, I casually remarked that perhaps I weakened the branch the half dozen or so times I had hit it.

So what does this have to do with the runaway horse? As I went to try to grab the horse's reins, he sauntered into the back yard, obviously confused and a bit scared at what was happening. He positioned himself between a fence, the hackberry, and this branch (which of course I hadn't yet removed from the ground), with his front left leg through the reins. Now, I don't know much about horses, but I know enough that this could trip the horse, which would be bad, particularly if I was in between equine and ground line.

I was able to grab the reins, leveraging the fallen limb to block his path of escape. As I carefully lifted the front left hock through them, I thought about how absolutely horrible it would feel if that foot opted to come down on my flimsy crocs. Of course I again found the hard path to a solution when an easier one existed, as my wife later reminded me that all I really needed to do was unbuckle the reins and lead by the two separate parts. No matter, horse was back in barn, in halter (I remembered at least to remove the bridle and put on a halter), tied to cross ties.

The entire escapade seemed to occur over about thirty minutes but in reality only lasted a few. After securing the horse, I ran back to our friend. Fortunately, she was convinced all she suffered was a hard bruise. She was grateful for my offer of ibuprofen and water, and I wished we had a bit of whisky to stop my shaking.

She explained that our horses were rather vocal when she had mounted hers, and that equine communication caused her horse to jerk backwards. That sudden movement kicked her leg out of the stirrup, and she fell as the startled horse trotted off. She was very happy (and I impressed) that I handled the runaway horse so well (although in all fairness he's very docile, and didn't seem to require any whisky).

After she left, sore but otherwise fine, physically and mentally, I returned to my "zone-out" watching Star Trek. I bet Captain Picard wouldn't have handled the runaway pony so well. "Make it so."

Thirty-Eight
Limp Along

Recently I completed running a half marathon (13.1 miles) in decent (for me) time, despite a minor foot injury. I try to do at least one long race per year, as the training helps me stay in shape. I think it is genetic, as my mother regularly runs 5Ks, 10Ks, marathons, even ultra-marathons. As long as she keeps running, I guess I can't quit – the "I'm too old" line doesn't hold water.

What does this have to do with horses? Horses and humans have something in common: legs. While they have four and we two, they perform the same purpose, movement at various speeds and directions. Well, using the word "speed" to describe my running is a stretch. I usually start slow and taper off.

You're still waiting for the equine connection, I know. A couple of days earlier, one of our horses had developed a rather pronounced limp. It was one of those injuries that even a semi-horse hobbyist (hobby horse?) like me could spot. She was definitely favoring one front leg over the other, as I did for much of the half-marathon due to my injury.

Why don't they (whomever "they" are) make crutches for horses? We humans are fortunate; injure a leg and you can compensate by extending your arms with wooden or medal appendages shoved into your armpits. Well, since horses have no arms, they can't use crutches. No arms equates to no armpits, which means no place to brace the crutches.

Anyway, my mare-maintainer wife had an idea as to the cause of the limp (horse's, not mine), and proceeded to fill a shallow bucket with a saltwater solution. This was to soak the hoof to help "blow the abscess." Yes, that does not sound terribly appealing, but the idea is if an abscess has developed in the hoof, it may eventually work itself out to relieve the pressure. The saltwater helps the process. As I type, I'm struggling to suppress the mental image of an abscess blowing.

This abscess thing was actually something I encountered, not personally but with another of the wife's ponies, several years ago. I had noticed an opened box of diapers in our truck. Now, for obvious reasons, this kind of freaked me out, since we had no children.

I walked to the barn to ask her about the diapers, figuring they were for a friend's toddler, but her duct taping a rather thick wad of white cloth like "stuff" to the hoof of her mare derailed my thoughts. "What's up with that?"

"She blew an abscess."

"Oh. I see. No, I don't. What does that mean?"

"She has an infection."

"What did you tape to the hoof?"

"It's a baby diaper, to keep the infection from getting worse and to help the healing process."

That explained the box in the truck. She went on to say that baby diapers make excellent blown abscess bandages. However, she was rather unsure of how to determine what size to buy. The store clerk wasn't much help when she asked what the baby's bottom's size was.

In a few short steps, we walked from running a race to horses using diapers. Now our horse did end up blowing the abscess and she healed rather fast, as did I. Even though my feet were also sore from running, I wasn't about to put diapers on them. Although if I did, I'd answer the clerk's question about diaper size by pointing to my foot and saying "Oh, about a 9 ½ wide."

Thirty-Nine
Cold Bale

Fall is a great time of year. With the changing colors of leaves, football, crisp days, and of course no need to mow the grass until spring, there's really not too much about fall that is negative. Except, of course, it leads to winter. You'd think that ten years of enduring Buffalo winters would have hardened me to subfreezing temperatures. Actually, I think I burned through a lifetime of cold resistance that decade.

As the trees dropped their final leaves and the first frost killed the last of my tomato plants, I knew that my nemesis was waiting for me figuratively (and soon literally) around the corner (of the barn). With winter approaching, I could not avoid the first round bale much longer.

Those who have followed this column over the years know that there are only a handful of horse chores I truly dread. Mowing the fields used to be up there, until the tractor came along. I reached the pinnacle of field mowing the day my neighbor warned me about my mower's exhaust pipe glowing. He spotted the anomaly from his deck as I rode blissfully ignorant of the impending danger, mowing a field of three-foot high grass (just a bit beyond its performance specifications). When I shut down the mower, the hot pipe started a small grass fire. Disco inferno!

My mowing experiences are much more pleasant now with the tractor use, and it is the dreaded round bales that sends fear up my spine every late fall. Superman has Lex Luthor, Batman has The Joker, and I have The Round Bales. You'd think that round bales are simply inanimate objects of dried field growth, and you'd be wrong. They have a life and a soul, and they are evil. They are obviously out to get me, probably because I burned some of their kin with the hot exhaust of a mower in the middle of a summer a few years ago.

I know horses like hay, and I understand good quality hay is necessary for maintaining horse health, but that doesn't change the fact that I dislike anything associated with moving hay. In the summer, it's tossing square bales up to the loft. We rely on using a combination of square and round bales, and since we don't have a place to store round bales (don't even suggest the loft) we buy them one or two at a time during the winter.

So on this particular cold morning, I felt a sense of angst. Just as our lab knows exactly when it's time for dinner, I know when it's round bale time. Sure enough, later that day my hay-haulin' honey called and asked me that dreaded question: "Can you push a round bale off the truck this evening? If so I'll pick one up."

You might assume that since a round bale is, well, round, it'd be easy to just roll off the flatbed of our truck – and you would be incorrect. Sometimes that is the case, but usually not. Often, the ball for the trailer hitch snags one of the bale's strings. It's not as if you can simply just lift it over the ball. Of course, the ponies tend to enjoy watching me rock it back and forth to get it unstuck. You'd think that they'd at least volunteer to come over and help, since it's their hay, anyway.

I have developed a system of sorts to unloading the round bale from the truck. The process involves bracing myself on the top of the crew cab and using my legs to push the bale away from the cab. Once I've gotten enough space between bale and cab, I wedge myself between them and again push. I have the strongest legs in the neighborhood now. Who needs a gym membership?

But I am getting older, of course. Each year I find it a bit more difficult to unload the round bale, so I've had to devise a different tactic. A couple of tie down straps, interlinked and wrapped around the hay, connected to either side of the front end loader works wonders. But I still like to do it the manual way, partially because I'm too lazy to get the tractor and straps in position but also I get an ego boost (and sometimes a charley horse) by pushing it off myself.

In any case, the hard work is worth it to keep the horses healthy and happy. I keep hoping they'll reciprocate just once by surprising me with a top sirloin, medium rare. For all the time I spend preparing their dinner, is asking for a nice one for me in return too much?

Forty
Muzzled

Recently we've taken in another rescue horse, and she is already well on the way to regaining her health. However, at least in the short term, we want to be 100% sure she doesn't have any medical issues that could affect our equine herd, so that means keeping her separate from our horses.

The regular mini-farm mini-herd has therefore taken up temporary around-the-clock residence in our front field. We don't have the horses graze in this field as often as others, and therefore it usually is pretty thick with lush grass. Our ponies know this, and virtually lick their chops in anticipation any time my wife or I even walk near the gate separating that field from their regular pasture. It is nature's all-you-can-eat buffet, and therein lies the problem.

We try to ensure our horses maintain a healthy weight, of course, but being grazers by nature horses will eat, and eat, and eat. An extended period in the lush field could very well mean that their girths wouldn't fit, but would probably make rolling in the field easier.

For the sake of maintaining proper equine health, we put feed muzzles on the ponies at night after their evening meal of grain. The devices don't prevent grass intake, but they do restrict the amount that can be eaten. Plus, they are easy to put on and take off . . . well, usually.

The majority of the mini-herd goes for the muzzle fairly easily as we manipulate the odds of such by putting a couple of treats in the muzzle. But the same isn't true for the ever sly appaloosa. No, getting her to come within ten feet of a muzzle is like getting me to enter a shopping mall.

Permit me to describe a typical muzzling ceremonial dance ritual. As I successfully place the apparatus on the percheron, the appaloosa is standing about twenty feet away, with her side to me, but watching closely what is going on. Sometimes it is difficult to see the whites of horses' eyes, but during "the dance" I can certainly see hers.

I calmly turn to the appaloosa, treats in one hand and on display and muzzle in the other and hidden behind my back, talking in a horse variation of English that I'm sure she can understand. She knows what's coming, and will let me get as close as about five feet before moving in the opposite direction. The appaloosa dictates that in this dance the female shall lead.

Enter the trees. This field is for the most part devoid of mature trees, save for two very old cedars growing side by side about ten feet apart almost dead center in the field. These twin cedars actually make for an excellent natural run in shed of sorts, and the ponies obviously consider it the central hang out spot You could call it the Starbucks of the field.

But there is no hanging out at the trees during the "Muzzle Shuffle." No, the trees provide the blocks and obstacles to prevent a successful muzzling. There is the classic "I'll go around the trees in front of you" as we circle each other, the sly "you can try to wait for me but I'll make it through the trees" maneuver, and the ever so popular "I'll wait for the others to come by and hide behind them and the trees" strategy.

There is a simple scientific principle, however, that always nullifies any exotic escape maneuver. In layman's terms, the attraction of a treat will always be stronger than the desire to defeat the muzzle. After a few minutes of dancing, the appaloosa gives into the dark side and accepts the treats . . . and the muzzle.

I firmly believe that she realizes that by limiting her intake we are helping her avoid temptation and preserve her healthy, beautiful figure. But I think she has a burning need bred from ego to prove to me that she is, in fact, letting me help her, and if she desired otherwise it would be her call.

Perhaps I should take a page out of this equine care manual and apply it to myself. At my last physical, my doctor nonchalantly mentioned I had gained a few pounds (as if I didn't already know that). Maybe I should borrow the appaloosa's muzzle for a while . . . at least when I go out to Shoney's.

Forty-One
Superheroes of the Pasture

This past weekend was essentially a guy's retreat, because my wife joined several of her girlfriends on a two-day trail ride a couple of hours away, leaving the guys alone at home. The guys, of course, are our two dogs and I. Our lab, definitely a mama's dog, pouted all weekend waiting for Mama to come home. Our Jack Russell Terrier, on the other hand, was very content to sit with Dad on the sofa for an afternoon of football and pizza.

My wife generally leaves extremely detailed horse care instructions whenever she's gone for more than a couple of hours. In all seriousness, she will write out these so even a dummy can't get it wrong. Never mind that I have before.

You'd think I'd have the instructions memorized by now, and generally I do. Simple tasks like ensuring they have enough water and the morning newspaper are easy. One thing I always seem to have a problem with, however, is fly control. Specifically, fly masks, or rather remembering to put fly masks on the ponies.

Fly masks are relatively simple constructs; mesh material form fitted to cover the horse's eyes while not coming close to touching them, with holes for the ears for stability, and secured with a Velcro strap. It is about impossible to mess up instructions to put them on the ponies, but then again, refer back to paragraph two.

It was the donkey that confused me, rather more precisely the donkey's mask. The coverings all have two holes (or so I thought), obviously for the ears. But as it was early on a Saturday morning, I had yet to have my coffee or Red Bull, and realized something was very wrong as I tried to put on the mask. At the risk of stating the obvious, donkeys have big ears. This particular fly mask has one big hole instead of two to accommodate the ears. Trust me, it is not there for the nose and mouth. Fortunately, our donkey was very patient and forgiving with me.

When the horses are together out in the field with their masks on, they remind me of superheroes defending the pasture. Think about it, most superheroes wore masks to disguise their identities, except for Superman. Those horn-rimmed glasses and slicked down hair really fooled everyone. Yeah, right, Clark. All other heroes had a more realistic approach to prevent identity theft or recognition – the trusty mask.

Thus, here in the field is this equine "Justice League," defending the pasture from evils emanating from external intrusions, to the electric fence shocks, to round bales attacking flanks. Being smaller, the donkey is sort of the sidekick of the group . . . think Robin to Batman. Batman's costume was testosterone-saturated black, but not Robin's – his was an ugly mix of red, aqua, and yellow. Let's not even discuss the tights. I explained to our donkey (remember, our equines understand us when we talk to them) that Robin always beat the crap out of the bad guys alongside Batman despite the duds. He seemed to take the superhero role to heart, terrorizing skunks that migrate into our fields. Do you have to ask how I can tell?

I feel somewhat comforted that these horse heroes are keeping us safe from all threats, yet I'm not sure why they need to hide their identities. You never see Bruce Wayne and Batman together, right? Pretty easy to draw conclusions about Batman's identity from that. Besides, our appaloosa's spots are very distinctive. Funny, though, I think yesterday I saw her trying on a pair of glasses. It won't work, despite what Clark says.

I should close by emphasizing they are not the only superheroes on our mini-farm. Our Jack Russell Terrier, when he isn't cheering on the Titans with me, is a cat terror. Every now and then, a stray cat will break through the equine defensive line. The Jack Russell is like the secondary, a safety that won't let a cat score.

And he doesn't wear a mask. Of course, the flies don't bother him anyway. They wouldn't dare.

Forty-Two
All Good Things . . .

Change is inevitable; it's what allows us to grow. Certainly, I can say I have changed greatly from a former city dweller from the north to a southerner running a mini-farm. If someone had told me ten years ago that I'd be bush hogging, and loving it, I'd have thought they were crazy. But change will do that to you.

With this chapter, I turn out the light in the loft, ending the *From the Loft* column. Over the years, I have written about many new experiences caring for horses and performing farm related duties, such as mowing fields prior to our purchase of a tractor, tossing up hay, and of course, tangling with my arch nemesis, the round bale. I'll admit, maybe some of the stories were embellished, perhaps even made up . . .

I have appreciated greatly the warm remarks and positive words I have received over the years about *From the Loft*. Such kind feedback provided much inspiration to write month after month. Knowing that my farm tales has entertained many is heartwarming.

But, as I said, change is inevitable. Sometimes it's for the good, sometimes not so good. But it's how we face change that allows us to grow. I could have resisted entering the equestrian life, but I'm glad I did not. I am definitely a much better person for it.

In closing, remember that as one door closes, another opens. As I embark on life changes of my own, I hold a deep faith that, as new doors open for me, I will continue to grow in ways I cannot imagine. Just as ten years ago I had no clue what a PTO was, I wonder what marvelous experiences the future holds. I am sure there will be many. Perhaps I'll finally finish that novel I've been working on for years.

www.ingramcontent.com/pod-product-compliance
Lightning Source LLC
Chambersburg PA
CBHW020616300426
44113CB00007B/659